Born to Spend

How to Overcome Compulsive Spending

Born to Spend

How to Overcome Compulsive Spending

Gloria
Arenson

 Human Services Institute
Bradenton, Florida

 **TAB BOOKS**
Blue Ridge Summit, PA

FIRST EDITION
FIRST PRINTING

© 1991 by **Gloria Arenson**
Published by HSI and TAB Books.
TAB Books is a division of McGraw-Hill, Inc.

Library of Congress Cataloging-in-Publication Data

Arenson, Gloria.
   Born to spend : how to overcome compulsive spending / by Gloria
Arenson.
     p. cm.
   Includes bibliographical references and index.
   ISBN 0-8306-2155-5 (p)
    1. Compulsive shopping.   2. Compulsive shopping—Treatment
I. Title.
RC569.5.S56A74   1991   91-14620
616.85′227—dc20   CIP

TAB Books offers software for sale. For information and a catalog, please
contact TAB Software Department, Blue Ridge Summit, PA 17294-0850.

The publication of this material does not imply affiliation with nor approval or
endorsement from Alcoholics Anonymous World Services, Inc., Narcotics
Anonymous World Services, Inc. or any other Twelve-Step Fellowship.

Questions regarding the content of this book should be addressed to:

Human Services Institute, Inc.
P.O. Box 14610
Bradenton, FL 34280

Acquisitions Editor: Kimberly Tabor
Development Editor: Lee Marvin Joiner, Ph.D.
Copy Editor: Pat Holliday
Cover Photography: Susan Riley, Harrisonburg, Virginia
Cover Design: Lori E. Schlosser

To Brock
My partner, teacher, and friend.

Books by Gloria Arenson

How to Stop Playing the Weighting Game

*A Substance Called Food: How to Understand,
Control and Recover From Addictive Eating*

Acknowledgments

I appreciate the cooperation of the wonderful people who have attended my classes and workshops. I thank my clients, people who are courageous in their determination to be free from compulsivity. I hope their stories will inspire others to follow in their footsteps.

The case histories are based on the lives of real people. I have disguised some facts to protect their confidentiality. Sometimes I have combined or simplified cases to present a point more clearly.

Compulsive spenders and debtors are members of both sexes. To remain nonsexist in my writing, I have used male and female pronouns interchangeably when speaking of people in a general sense.

Contents

COMPULSIVE SPENDING:

A NATION IN DENIAL

1

SPENDING
IN PURSUIT OF HAPPINESS

One morning several years ago I happened to turn on my television set to the public television station. A man was standing in front of an audience talking with great passion about unhappy families and compulsion. I quickly became mesmerized by his charismatic manner and found myself reaching for paper and pen to take notes.

The man was John Bradshaw, a man with valuable new insights. Bradshaw, himself a recovered alcoholic and an adult child of an alcoholic, explained addiction and compulsion in a very broad sense, including not just alcohol or drugs but all types of compulsive behaviors. His ideas helped me to formulate a new approach to my work.

For over twenty years I have concentrated on helping people with the problems of eating disorders. As I worked with more people through the years, I began to realize that there was a common denominator in all eating disorders, the compulsive urge. Compulsive overeaters have the urge to binge, bulimics binge and purge, while anorexics sometimes binge but mostly have the compulsion to starve.

I have written two other books, *How to Stop Playing the Weighting Game* and *A Substance Called Food: How to Understand, Control, and Recover from Addictive Eating*. In them I explained the process of compulsive urges, what they mean, and how they can be controlled. During the years I was creating a new approach to these problems, I was aware that at least sixty percent of my clients were sober alcoholics, usually in Twelve-Step programs for drugs or alcohol. They had given up the deadlier addictions, but they were stuck in the thrall of food.

As time passed I began to notice that many of these people were also compulsive spenders and debtors. They usually did not talk at first about these behaviors, not because of shyness but because they didn't consider them much of a problem compared to alcohol, drugs, food, and "love too much" relationships.

Many people call themselves "compulsive personalities" although science maintains that there is no such thing. What John Bradshaw said really hit me. I felt as if a light bulb had truly come on in my head! I knew that the problem is not alcohol, drugs, food, shopping, sex, exercise, or smoking. These are the solutions. The real problem is that most of us do not know how to cope with the ups and downs of our lives. We run away from discomfort and mask our pain and fear with temporary escape or longer-term oblivion. We keep doing this until the solution becomes a full-fledged problem with a life of its own.

When many of my eating disorder clients stopped compulsively binging or purging, they often turned to other compulsions. I remember a woman who began to get her eating under control and then resumed smoking after having given it up for years. She had begun to work in the family business. Her father was her boss. Besides job stress, many relationship issues were coming into her consciousness. She was terribly angry and frustrated. Instead of dealing with her real problems, she smoked.

Another binge/purger began to buy clothing, six of a kind at once, after she quit stuffing with food. Other clients revealed that they resorted to different compulsive urges at different times. Paul overate most of the time, but when he was emotionally distraught he sought sex compulsively. Norma Jean binged or shopped. Stephanie got drunk, used drugs, drank huge amounts of coffee, loved too much, binged and purged, smoked, and spent.

I call the switching from one compulsive act or substance to another the "Hierarchy of Compulsions." It became evident to me that the urge to binge or splurge in some way was the outward evidence of inner turmoil. The type of spree depended on the personal style of the binger. Cora was a compulsive who decided to study her personal style. Here is the chart she created. The first column shows the intensity of her

Compulsive Spending: A Nation in Denial

anxiety on a scale of one to ten. The second column denotes the activity or substance she begins to abuse. The third column explains the feelings she is trying to push down or avoid. Notice that the most common feelings that put her out of control are anger, helplessness, and a sense of being overwhelmed.

CORA'S COMPULSIVE BEHAVIORS

Anxiety	Activity	Feelings
10	Spending	Hurt, Helpless
10	Changing things in house or relationship	Anger, Loss
9	Listmaking	Overwhelmed
8	Workaholism	Loss, Anger
8	Eat, read, TV, all at once	Helpless, Overwhelmed
8	Wash & wax floor	Intensely helpless
7	Movies and popcorn	Frustration, Overwhelmed
6	Hobbies	Anger, Overwhelmed
6	Gardening	Helpless, Loss
6	Washing dishes	Out of control
5	Sex	Anger, Overwhelmed
5	Nail biting	Inadequate, Tense
4	Fantasizing change	Loss
4	Cutting toenails	Tense, Helpless
4	Relationship connecting	Loss, Fear of "the void"
3	Overeat ice cream	Anger, Abandoned
2	Phoning	Lonely inner child

4

2	Reading	*Overwhelmed, Anger*
1	Television	*Overwhelmed*

Among the first people I counseled when I began in private practice was a young woman I'll call Zoe. I thought of Zoe as a "triple threat" person. She vacillated between alcohol, drugs and food. One day she discovered that what she really wanted was to "zone out." She just wanted to lose consciousness and not feel the pain of living. Her first choice was to use drugs. She had overdosed twice. When she was off drugs, she usually would drink until she passed out. Food was a poor third, but very available.

Zoe worked hard to overcome her three compulsive urges. Although she did stop using hard drugs and was able to control her food cravings and lose weight, alcohol was still a "sometimes" thing. Zoe never could free herself of all three addictive behaviors at once. One major decision that Zoe made because of reevaluating her life and changing her perspective through counseling was to move away to a less stressful environment. When Zoe left town she was free of drugs and had lost weight. Her alcohol abuse had lessened.

About a year later I received a letter from Zoe in which she reported that she had gone to an alcoholism counselor in her determination to achieve health. The counselor had recommended that the most important thing was to be free of booze, and nothing else mattered. So Zoe gained thirty-five pounds! She was extremely frustrated because she knew that although she was sober, she was still drunk with food.

It became clear to me that Zoe and millions of others keep doing the same thing, switching from one substance or behavior to another. These people, their counselors, doctors and families believe that they are cured of their unacceptable addiction, but the truth is that it has just been transformed to something less dramatic.

I have spoken with many licensed therapists and have presented my views at centers and agencies where the belief is that alcohol and drugs are the real problems. In recent years, the eating disorders—anorexia nervosa and bulimia—are being recognized as major evidences of dysfunction, but other behaviors like compulsive spending are not. We must stop compartmentalizing these behaviors.

In my private practice I began to concentrate on the problems of spending and debting as inadequate solutions to life problems, besides the other well-known addictions. I began to teach classes and formed small groups to help people work through their "acting out" with money.

I discovered that two kinds of people attended. One group was the people already in Twelve-Step organizations, usually Alcoholics Anonymous and Overeaters Anonymous. These people were in touch with the way they turned to pleasurable substances to dull their pain. Some had joined Debtors Anonymous and continued to see the problem of spending and debting as a disease. The second group was men and women who didn't seem caught up in other major addictions, but were secretly worried about the way they overspent or binged by buying or charging.

The common denominator for all of them was that using money or credit was a way of letting off emotional steam, a distraction from their daily problems. They were not facing their problems head on, not processing their feelings, not *resolving* their problems, just running away from or postponing them. Many Twelve-Step people were so intent on keeping their sobriety that they didn't realize that behaviors such as spending, jogging, cleaning, reading, masturbating, watching soap operas, or gardening had become as addictive as substances like tobacco, alcohol, drugs and food.

The first stumbling block I encountered in my work was the widely-held belief that compulsive shopping and debting isn't a serious problem. We joke about it when we say, "When the going gets tough, the tough go shopping." Many people, including some health professionals, do not understand how these compulsions can be linked to other psychological problems.

The second obstacle is the theory that all addictive and compulsive behaviors are diseases. Dr. Stanton Peele has stated that America has now entered the Age of Addiction. "What characterizes modern-day Americans and American society that can possibly explain the out-of-control growth of the experience of being out of control?" In his book, *Diseasing of America*, Dr. Peele maintains that we are bombarded by the media, and the concepts of addiction as a disease are being marketed as if they are products. We hear it so often we eventually come to believe it. Another factor is that we have distanced ourselves from our basic emotional and physical experiences by creating a picture of the world and others around us as a fearsome place. A third possibility is that we live in a very medicalized society. We tend to rely on technical solutions to sickness and other problems.

We have become convinced that we are helpless. We believe the medical model of disease: we didn't create it, therefore, we can't cure it. Only professional healthcare experts can fix us. Meanwhile we must hope that a cure can be found, but are not required to take responsibility for our actions (the Twinkie defense).

It is bigger than we are, so only something bigger can save us or cure us. I don't mean to be blasphemous nor to discount the amazing results of the Twelve-Step programs, but I have often wondered why God can't cure alcoholism, overeating, drugs, and gambling if God is so all-powerful that He created heaven and earth? The members of anonymous groups think of themselves as having a lifelong disease that can never be cured. They must bear the label of victim forever. Recovery is only a daily reprieve. The impact of labeling an activity as a disease often convinces people that they cannot control these experiences. Dr. Alan Marlatt did a classic study with alcoholics where they drank more when they believed that they were drinking alcohol than when they actually drank alcohol in a disguised form. Their *beliefs* caused the lack of control, not the substance.

A student in a class for compulsive eaters complained that she couldn't eat just one slice of pizza and stop. The second week of class she revealed that she had eaten *one* corn chip and stopped. The class oohed in amazement, seeming to imply "How could she have achieved that almost impossible feat?"

I used to ask my clients who were members of diet clubs whether anyone went home with them to police their actions. "Who kept you good?" I asked. The answer is "*You do!*" Who chose to eat one corn chip and stop? By the eighth week of class that student could choose to eat one slice of pizza and stop. She stopped feeling powerless and learned how to manage her life and her behavior.

I began to apply the program for change that I had created for compulsive eaters and purgers to spenders and debtors. They had the same wonderful success. The spenders began to understand what set them off, and grew more conscious and responsible about both their feelings and their behaviors. I will be repeating throughout this book that the behaviors of spending and debting are not the real problem. The underlying problem is that most of us don't know how to solve the life problems arising from stressful situations and relationships. Compulsive urges to shop and to have "things" are ways we distract ourselves from our real issues and our intense negative feelings.

In the following chapters I will teach you how to overcome compulsive spending and debting using this approach.

AWARENESS: Stop rationalizing.

ACCEPTANCE: Understand that you are not a bad person. You will discover that you do what you do for reasons that make sense when you consider what elements or experiences have shaped you.

ACTION: Learn new ways to think about yourself and new ways to behave.

Living a life out-of-balance is not a disease. The behaviors we develop to try to feel good again are not the result of disease. They are "syndromes," a set of concurrent emotions or actions that form an identifiable pattern. Thinking you have a disease prevents you from being responsible for yourself. You can rationalize, "I can't help myself." I want you to know the answer is within, and so is the power to bring your life into balance.

2

WHO SPENDS ?

Spenders and debtors come in many sizes, shapes, and economic groups. Some go on shopping sprees but manage to pay their debts and live within their means. Others live well beyond their means and stay one step ahead of their creditors. Some spenders have gone to jail for passing bad checks and many have had to declare bankruptcy.

Not all spenders abuse money or credit for the same reasons. They adopt different styles of spending and encourage themselves with various rationalizations that make their behavior seem normal and desirable. Over the years I have met many types of people who use money compulsively. Let me introduce a few.

THE SUPERPERSON

These people are the saviors of others in need. They often give away all they have to aid worthy causes. Stan was a successful businessman who complained, "I keep giving, but I can't seem to get rid of it!" Stan's mother spent money on others, not on herself. Stan decided that when you spend money on others, you are showing them love. When he goes on clothes buying binges he tells himself,"I must love myself because I bought that for me." Mostly Stan gives large sums to charity.

Olivia found herself frittering away an inheritance. She couldn't resist helping people who told her hard luck stories. She had been brought up to believe that it was important to be altruistic and that a good person gives to those who are in need. Because she secretly believed that she didn't deserve to be better than most people, she forgot to take care of her needs first.

CINDERELLA

Cinderellas are usually women I think of as the "genteel poor." They often are very intelligent and creative, but seem unable to earn enough money to do more than get by. They usually spend all they have anyway because they expect to be rescued by Prince Charming. Most of these people are taken in or helped by others who provide food, shelter, and even fancy vacation trips.

Selma was a Cinderella "self-debtor." A self-debtor is someone who punishes herself by not spending money on herself. Selma had suffered severe abuse as a child. So she thought of herself as unworthy. She was married to a prince of a man who earned large sums of money. He loved to buy her expensive gifts. Selma rarely bought herself anything. When she shopped, it was in the bargain basement or only at a sale.

Loretta was a different kind of Cinderella. She made lots of money but constantly felt like a drudge —having a high pressure job besides running a house and bringing up two teenagers. Loretta escaped from her chores through constant shopping binges. She rationalized that she needed to get away from her housework, and besides, she was often buying things for her husband and children. When the balance got too high on one charge card, Loretta simply changed stores. Every month she agonized over how to pay off her debts by juggling credit cards.

Toni was a "Secondhand Rose." Her home was jam packed with THINGS, all purchased in thrift stores and swap meets. "I have to have that thing and my life will be miraculously changed." Toni excuses herself by explaining,"I only spent eight dollars instead of eighty dollars." But by spending steadily and compulsively, she has used up all the money she was saving to put herself through school. Toni's mother loved things too, but forbade buying anything that wasn't new. Mom was a spender and dad was thrifty and saved everything. Toni realizes that her craving for used goods is also a reflection of her anger toward a mother who wasn't nurturing, a way of getting even. And it is a way of identifying with her father.

UNDESERVING POOR

In the play *My Fair Lady*, when Henry Higgins tries to give Eliza Dolittle's father ten pounds he refuses the gift. Dolittle explains that he is one of the "undeserving poor," and he wants to stay that way. Accepting ten pounds would make him too respectable; five pounds would be better because he could squander it and not feel guilty.

Eleanor, a woman in her fifties, was struggling to recover from addictions to alcohol and food when I met her. She lived from hand to mouth and complained that her dilapidated car was about to break down for good. "Mother said that my hand was a sieve," she announced. Eleanor spends whatever comes her way, often buying three or four of a product, usually to give to others. She remains poor.

Eleanor's mother was the same way, a self-debtor, who often wore her daughter's underwear. Father, a prosperous businessman, always carried a bankroll of thousands of dollars in cash, which he freely gave away as loans. He spent all that he earned. Eleanor combines the traits of both her parents, acting self-denying like mother and being generous and spending all she has, like father. Eleanor and her father had a stormy relationship. He had a series of heart attacks, which finally killed him, but Eleanor often blames herself for causing his death because of her angry behavior. Being poor and staying miserable is one way she inflicts punishment for this imaginary crime.

THE REBEL

Spending was a temper tantrum for Dave. Dave was raised in a very small town. During his teen years, he began to rebel. Unlike his friends who began to drink beer as a sign of their rebellion, Dave decided to be different and turned to marijuana.

His parents were constantly complaining that they couldn't make ends meet. "We can't afford it" was their theme song. Dave grew up with these messages:

- Money is something we never have enough of.
- Borrowing is bad.
- Second rate is good enough for us.
- Don't flaunt money.
- Good quality is important, but luxury is for others.
- We can get by without.

Dave hung around with many kids from affluent homes. He became more and more frustrated that he couldn't have what they did. He rationalized, "I'm as good as the next guy. Why not spend?" His fury toward his parents who tried to live within their means led to a life of compulsive spending and debting as money burned a hole in Dave's pocket.

THE STATUS SEEKER

These people use money to impress others. Sometimes they come from poor families and spend compulsively to create a life they never had. Others simply spend everything they have to buy designer clothing and go on fancy vacations.

Debby told herself that she *needed* all the expensive clothes she purchases. She was dating a man whose lifestyle included going out often to posh and trendy places where people kept up with the latest in fashion fads. She had to look right to be accepted.

Connie was used to living in style. Her parents treated her like a princess. Dad used to reassure her,"You never have to worry." So she stopped worrying. In fact, Connie used shopping as an antidote for fear. Spending kept her feelings at bay. And Connie loved to live the "good life." Besides expensive clothing, she indulged herself in jewelry and hoarded gourmet food products. She spent thousands of dollars dining in the finest restaurants. She kept up the front of the wealthy, carefree, career girl. As long as she had cash in her wallet she felt rich. Connie told herself that credit cards weren't real, and since there was some money in the bank, she could charge as much as she wanted. Yet there was never enough.

THE MAGICAL CHILD

Gail and Gary were binge buddies who assuaged each others' guilt over compulsive charging. When they were in desperate straits and faced with bankruptcy, Gail asked Gary what they should do. He replied, "Let's hang in there and pray to God." The magical child prefers to deny reality and fantasize that others will take care of his future in some fabulous or miraculous way. These people often binge with money to obliterate the pain of their fears of the future or of their inadequacy.

When Gary lost his job, he persuaded Gail to rent a larger house as a symbol that the money would come. This can be seen as "When my ship comes in" mentality. Gary liked to live and spend as if his ship was already in port.

One variation on this theme is the "Scarlett O'Hara" woman who keeps rationalizing, "I'll worry about paying for that tomorrow." Jessica kept telling herself this until she got the final notice that her utilities were about to be shut off.

Hannah spent money to surprise the child within. She was a compulsive catalogue shopper and credit card junkie. She loved getting packages. It was a treat for her little girl self, like Christmas every few days. The little girl didn't worry about how to pay. Hannah would just juggle her credit cards and hope for the best.

THE DAREDEVIL

Richard loved to live life "on the edge." He ran a large business, and held his breath each month when the payroll was due, fearful he wouldn't have enough to pay his employees. He lived in an expensive home and generally enjoyed a rich lifestyle.

Jennifer also spent every cent that came to her. She was filled with anxiety each month, fearing that she couldn't pay her bills. She hated the anxious moments, but found that there was a kind of thrill to the suspenseful situation. Jennifer recognized that her parents lived this way too, and she was recreating their behavior.

THE DUMMY

Dummies never balance their checkbooks. They keep wondering where all their money went, yet they really don't want to know. If you know how much money you spend, on what, and how much is left, you must take responsibility for your actions. Many people rely on their banks to let them live beyond their credit by using the overcharge. Connie, Debbie, and Gary often did this.

Although I am punctilious about balancing my check book, I have been battling a "dummy" behavior all my life. I pride myself on being a good comparison shopper and wise consumer, yet whenever I make a large purchase like a water heater, TV, new roof, or new plumbing, I immediately forget how much it costs. At the same time I can tell you exactly how much tomatoes cost in the supermarket and the difference in price in margarine from last week to this week.

When I was six, I asked my father how much money he earned. I will never forget his rage as he replied, "THAT IS NONE OF YOUR BUSINESS!" His command was so powerful that I have to make any expenditure I consider to be part of a "man's" world "none of my business." I am such an obedient daughter that I simply wipe all knowledge of dollars and cents out of my mind to this day.

THE INDULGER

Marie didn't feel loved as a child. As she grew up and started earning money, she became the indulgent mother she never had. "I love myself by buying things for myself. I just keep charging," she said. Marie also indulged her desires for rich foods and cigarettes. She was battling both compulsive overeating and compulsive spending.

Lupe indulged herself through constant shopping. She rarely went on spending sprees, but loved finding bargains and got excited at the challenge of finding things below full price. Her rationalization was that she wasn't really spending much money all at once, although she frequently bought the same item in three different colors because one wasn't enough. Lupe grew up in a middle-class family where her father handled the money and was a good provider. Yet it was Lupe's mother who seemed to have the most influence. Mother always felt poor because her family had lost their land during the Great Depression of the thirties.

Mother agonized over spending money, shopping only at sales and not buying things for herself.

"It had to be a special occasion to get things. We weren't poor yet I felt denied. I was told that *things* weren't important," explained Lupe. One of the worst memories of her childhood, which convinced Lupe she was different and poor, was that her mother made her wear the same dress to school two days in a row. Her mother wanted to make sure the dresses were dirty before she washed them, but little Lupe only remembers the embarrassment it caused her.

NOT GOOD ENOUGH

Matt described himself as someone who eats too much, loves too much and spends too much. His parents often told him that he wasn't a good boy, and he was cheating them because he wasn't what they expected him to be. He decided "I'm not good enough."

Matt's mother was from a family with a poverty consciousness. She continued to reinforce this negative outlook through self-debting behaviors and complaints. Her favorite words were "You can't . . .." She raised Matt alone until he was eight, and there was never enough. Matt's stepfather was a good provider but let the boy know that finances were none of his business. Matt continued to feel poor. Although his family had nice things, they seemed the last ones on the block to get them.

As a debtor with bill collectors knocking on the door, Matt created a lifestyle in which this message was constantly being reinforced. It proved that he wasn't good enough or didn't have enough. Matt kept borrowing from the future to pay off the past. The pattern of spending and debting justified his unworthiness.

POOR LITTLE RICH GIRL

Sybil had grown up after World War II in a wealthy family where women spent most of their time doing good works in the community and life was pleasant. "I think the first two words I learned were *charge it*," she said. Women were treated like children, given an allowance and never taught about investing, earning, or acting responsible with money. And so, Sybil grew up as a "dummy." She didn't know how much money she had. She didn't feel compelled to work for money because it just kept coming to her.

Today Sybil lacks money. Since she never gave it a thought and simply "blew it" without making it work for her future, she is broke. Yet she still lives like a woman of means, either doing volunteer work like the women in her mother's generation did, or taking jobs that pay almost nothing, because she is afraid of the workaday world—the responsibilities of a real job. She was protected and ignored. The result has been a devastating naivete that keeps her helpless and depressed.

THE NEEDY GREEDY CHILD

Cora, at age forty-nine, was battling many compulsions. Scarcity of money in her childhood set the stage for her money woes, yet there was no real shortage. Cora's mother, a divorced woman, sent Cora to live with her grandmother. Cora's mother earned an excellent salary and sent money for Cora's upkeep, but grandma never used it for Cora. Instead she thriftily saved it and later returned it.

As a result, Cora never received the treats and nice things that money could provide. She felt needy and acted greedy with money, sweets, and sex as an adult. Empty cupboards meant scarcity and reminded Cora of her unhappy early years. "I have to fill them, but then I feel guilty about spending. I want to budget yet can't because I need *plenty*."

Cora spends money to "pass as middle-class." Because of her blue-collar family experience with grandma, she believes that you have to "look right" to be accepted. "I can get into an alcoholic high buying clothes," she says. So Cora spends more than she can afford with credit cards to the max and bounced checks to rectify.

An unusual part of Cora's story is the influence of her grandfather. Grandfather hid his money in his cabin and was murdered for it. Cora's mother was known to salt away her money compulsively, but Cora believes, "He hid his money, but it didn't help. If I don't spend all my money, it will get taken away."

THE SPOILED BRAT

Diane loves to shop. When she runs out of money or feels too guilty to charge, she sometimes steals small items. At those times, the feeling that she just has to have it is so strong that she feels powerless to stop. Like a small child, she cannot postpone the gratification. If she can't have it she has a temper tantrum and tells herself that she deserves it at all costs.

Diane was treated like a princess by her parents who have never said *no* to her. Not only could she have whatever she wanted, often clothes and objects were presented to her before she could even wish for them. Diane's mother, herself a compulsive shopper, seemed to read her daughter's mind and, like a wonderful fairy godmother, produce lovely things, anticipating her desires.

Since Diane grew up with no limitations, she doesn't know how to set limits for the needy greedy child within who craves clothing, food, and good feelings. She often has troubles in relationships because she expects those close to her to read her mind and automatically provide her with whatever she wants, as her mother did.

Although each person I have described abuses money or credit differently, they all act compulsively and irresponsibly, caught up in the rationalizations they have lived with for years. Yet each has revealed their story to me because their behavior has caused them so much pain that they no longer want to remain in denial. Perhaps you have identified with one or more of them. In the following chapters I will help you understand why you do what you do and how you can stop.

3

CAUSES
OF COMPULSIVE
SPENDING AND DEBTING

What is compulsion? How is it possible to understand this behavior? Why do so many people feel like slaves to their urges to spend and live beyond their means? Compulsion is loss of control and a continuation of the behavior despite harmful consequences. In other words, *if you cannot control when you start or stop an activity, you have a problem!*

John Bradshaw, well-known authority on addictive behaviors, defines compulsion as "a mood altering event, experience, or thing, which brings major life problems." You may be able to pay your bills, but if you hate what you do with money and are unable to change your behaviors or control buying binges and urges to spend, you are acting compulsively.

Compulsive spending and debting is not a primary problem. It is a solution to other problems. Eventually the urges to spend and debt take on a life of their own and seem overwhelming. Spenders suffer from anxiety, depression and remorse, yet seem powerless to stop.

Compulsive urges to shop and spend may arise as a reaction to feelings of deprivation and a desire for instant gratification, but it is also the inadequate coping mechanism of many people whose lives are filled with stress and loneliness. Buying things or using money to create pleasurable experiences is a temporary way to feel good and masks emotions such as pain, anger, anxiety, fear, or depression. Getting high on shopping is a way to distract yourself from your real feelings.

Here is a list of common excuses for spending that I have collected from compulsive people:

- I deserve it!
- I may not be able to have it later.
- I need it. I WANT it.
- You only live once. Go for it!
- It was on sale.
- It will make me feel better.
- Everyone else has one . . . why not me?
- I like the way people react when I buy six at once.
- It's normal for people to have a . . . (car, VCR, car phone).

DON'T FEEL BAD, FEEL GOOD

Most of us fear pain, either physical or emotional. We try to avoid it at all costs, or, if we can't, we devise ways to lessen the discomfort. If you study billboards, advertisements and commercials, you will find that we are constantly being told *"Don't worry; be happy."* We are encouraged to buy things or eat, drink, or medicate ourselves to not feel anxious, frustrated, or uncomfortable. As a result, we tend to seek immediate relief and gratification. Getting high or spending to get pleasure objects can be so enjoyable that you may tell yourself, "If one is good, more is better." This kind of thinking is likely to lead to compulsive acting out of your cravings or urges. Credit is easily available and can be used to buy pleasure producing substances like alcohol, drugs and food or objects like cars, clothes and furnishings or to purchase pleasurable experiences.

Compulsion results from the constant use of comfort through eating, drinking, spending, getting high, or being sexual. We use them as Band-Aids for minor injuries. It is as if a person with an ulcer refuses to see a doctor, and, instead, self-medicates with antacids that produce only temporary relief. The underlying condition doesn't get cured and continues to flare up.

When you apply the same remedy, compulsive spending or debting, for a long time, a new problem may arise. The pleasurable moment of spending or shopping can take on a life of its own. The original painful situation or relationship that caused the anxiety, resentment, or fear is still there, and now there is an additional worry—how to curb your compulsive spending binges.

In our culture we tend to accept dysfunctional behavior as normal when it is widespread. We use phrases like "everyone does it" to keep from feeling guilty. Sometimes we act like sheep, just following along, taking the path of least resistance. The word "denial" is frequently used in alcohol or drug therapy. It means that many of us know better, but don't want to face the truth because of the responsibilities we will have to accept or the fears we will have to face.

We also fear that if we "blow the whistle" or "rock the boat," others will point out our faults or punish us, so we just keep still and go along with the crowd. This is why we elect politicians who cheat and lie to us, and contribute to churches run by religious leaders who act hypocritically or criminally. Although a part of us knows, we just continue to pretend it isn't that bad.

How do we deal with this hypocrisy? We tune out; we turn away; we avoid. Finally, we forget, and we forget we have forgotten. One way to tune out is to shop or spend.

Most of the people in our society feel that way about spending. Everyone can get credit cards; lots of them. We joke about being "credit card junkies" without being fully aware that abusing credit and spending is another kind of addiction for millions. We tell each other that it doesn't count and isn't really a problem. Alcohol and drugs are the *real* issues.

I believe that the real issue is not alcohol, drugs, food, sex, smoking, or spending. The real issue is the horror of realizing how far millions of us will go to avoid feeling bad when life is hard. Compulsive spending is simply another way to get high. Most compulsive spenders also abuse substances like alcohol and food. They simply switch from one to the other.

ADDICTION TO FEELINGS

In their compelling book, *Craving for Ecstacy*, Harvey Milkman and Stanley Sunderwirth explain that human beings crave three kinds of feelings: (1) relaxation; (2) excitement; and (3) fantasy or oblivion. You and I seem to prefer one of these sensations more than the others, sometimes to such a degree that we invent amazing ways to produce this feeling to replace the discomfort or anxiety in our lives.

People who prefer relaxation often pleasure themselves by overeating carbohydrates, TV watching, drinking alcohol, or using tranquilizers. They enjoy the mellow, laid-back feeling they can create for themselves and look in amazement at people who adore roller coasters and thrills. People who enjoy feeling aroused or excited are frequently drawn to skydiving, race car driving, caffeine, cocaine, horror movies and compulsive spending. Another segment of the population wants to feel oblivious to their surroundings and problems. They learn to use anesthetic or psychedelic drugs or sleep. I have known people who literally get lost in a good book. You may speak to them, but they don't hear you. They lose all awareness of their surroundings. Computer addicts also lose track of time as they become mesmerized by their machines. Meditation is a wonderful process for altering your state of mind to reach another plane of awareness, but some people don't know how to create that experience in a healthy or natural way.

The idea that we tend to become addicted to feelings rather than substances explains why so many people call themselves "compulsive personalities." Many sober alcoholics still smoke packs of cigarettes a day, drink many cups of coffee and crave sweets. Eating disorder sufferers frequently shoplift or spend compulsively.

Most human beings seem to favor one feeling more than the others, and compulsive people often turn to behaviors or substances that will bring them down when they are too high or lift them up when they are too low. Thus, many compulsive eaters are also compulsive spenders. Food often acts as a depressant and shopping as a form of arousal or excitement.

BRAIN CHEMISTRY IS A KEY

Drs. Milkman and Sunderwirth maintain that adult compulsions result from a combination of painful childhood experiences, a genetic predisposition toward compulsivity, and negative pressures created by the society we live in. They have discovered that the reason some people prefer relaxation while others crave excitement or fantasy may be based on differences in our brain chemistry.

Electrical activity in certain areas of the brain is responsible for feelings of pleasure and pain. Self-induced changes in brain neurotransmitters can lead to addictive behavior. Compulsive individuals repeat specific behaviors that cause activity in the brain nerve cells and create intense feelings. Different behaviors or substances lead to different sensations. This tendency toward addictive or compulsive preferences can even be recognized in some people in early childhood.

A chemical called *serotonin* is created in the brain and plays an important role in mood changes. Studies have compared the brain chemistry of people who died of natural causes with those who committed suicide. The results show that those who took their own lives had much lower levels of serotonin. Lack of serotonin can affect your mood, producing irritability.

COMPULSION AND THE FAMILY

Research into the mind-body connection and how it influences our behavior is exciting. Still, a predisposition toward compulsivity does not guarantee that a person will suffer from a compulsive disorder. A most important factor interacting with an individual's biology and environment is childhood experience.

Compulsive Spending: A Nation in Denial

Some families provide an unhealthy environment for a child. Let me describe four kinds of dysfunctional families. If you were reared in one of these family types, you may still be suffering from the damage of your unhappy upbringing. They are: (1) Overachieving, (2) Judgmental, (3) Enmeshed, and (4) Distant. You may identify with traits of more than one of these family systems. An outcome of growing up in one of these families is that you don't learn how to solve problems effectively and don't get a chance to learn how healthy people relate to each other. Because you did not receive enough healthy nurturing and acceptance, you may have formed false beliefs about yourself based on your unfortunate experiences. These false ideas lead you to behave in ways that feel phony and cause you unhappiness or stress.

PRESSURE TO ACHIEVE

The overachieving family judges its members by their successes. John Bradshaw describes these people as "human doings" instead of "human beings." The overachieving family pressures the child to do great things and keep doing. Never be satisfied! Set new goals! Keep striving! Each family defines success in a different way. In my family, success for women meant to be married to a successful man who made lots of money. It meant having lovely clothes and plenty of material possessions. In Bonnie's home, success meant being a college graduate.

Children who grow up in a family that pressures to achieve often hear these phrases: "Be good." "Make us proud of you." The child is supposed to already that the rules for being good are: (1) a good child gets good grades; (2) a good child never gets into trouble; (3) a good child is careful not to hurt anyone's feelings; and, of course, (4) a good child never gets angry. Appearances matter greatly in overachieving families where the motto is "What will other people think?"

Adults who were brought up in this striving atmosphere often tend to be highly self-critical and condemn themselves if they do not live up to the impossible standards they set for themselves. They don't realize that these are irrational and unreachable goals. The family is like a planet; its environment was the only model of the world available to them. As adults these damaged children are unable to accept compliments or to like themselves for any wonderful talents and traits they already possess. They secretly believe that none of these things count because they aren't perfect enough yet.

WHEN WILL I BE GOOD ENOUGH?

Children who come from a judgmental family constantly hear what is wrong with them, but rarely are praised or told what is right with them. Critical parents abuse their children physically, verbally, or emotionally. These ignorant people believe that their children should know they love them, so they don't have to keep saying it. Instead they frequently discount and ridicule. This makes the child feel small and helpless. She begins to believe that no matter what she does it won't be good enough. She can't get her needs met, no matter how hard she tries.

Caroline was an unwanted child of a teenage mother. Her grandparents took care of her. They made sure she had food and clothing, but Caroline was pretty much ignored. No one smiled at her or played with her. Caroline's family was not verbally critical. Their neglect of her spirit made her think that there was something bad about her. As an adult she became compulsive about buying and having *things*. When she looked at her house packed with furniture and works of art, she temporarily felt okay. For a moment she had the fantasy home she always wished for. But it didn't last, and then she craved more and more. When I first met Caroline, she and her husband were buying a new house. Their old house had become too small for all her belongings, and still she hungered.

We have all known people who are intelligent and creative, yet settle for a life of mediocrity and quiet despair. They have given up the struggle to be perfect. Many of these people are the product of overly judgmental parents. Others seem outwardly confident and successful, but tell themselves they are frauds and keep away from intimate relationships in which others might find out the truth about their guilt.

In the last chapter I described Gail and Gary who were "binge buddies." Unhappily, Gary's nickname in his family was "Stupid." He grew up with a stepfather who resented him and was jealous of Gary's relation-ship with his mother. Gary tried hard to succeed, but each time his star seemed on the ascendant he sabo-taged himself. He went from job to job, always finding an excuse to quit or get fired. Each time he was down and out his family would loan him money. As he got back on his feet they would find fault with him and criticize. The message that was unconsciously rein-forced was "Be a loser and we'll love you."

Children who are parented by angry or critical parents hear these phrases: "Don't do as I do, do what you're told." "Don't ask questions." They are taught not to feel their feelings when they hear: "There's nothing to be afraid of," "I'll give you something to cry about," "Don't feel bad," or "It's not nice to be angry with your brother." This kind of family doesn't allow you to be youself because the you that's you is not what pleases them. A typical misconception is that feeling sad or crying is a sign of weakness, so don't have these feelings. Anger is a "no-no."

If you aren't allowed to feel what you feel, where do the feelings go? You bury them. Some people learn to eat, drink, or use drugs to stuff them down. Others shop to comfort themselves with substitute feel-goods of material possessions.

WHOSE LIFE DO I LIVE?

Another term for the clinging family is "enmeshed." Many of my clients who are products of extremely clingy families often tell me that they come from a "close family." They have been brainwashed to believe that they are "all for one and one for all." An outsider looking at an enmeshed group may think they are one big happy family, but they aren't. Each member is a slave to the idea that it is "us against them," or "united we stand; divided we fall." Adults who came from a clinging family often feel misunderstood, ganged up on, and invaded.

Debby, the young woman who had to have lots of fancy clothes, came from a family that constantly reminded her that "family are the only ones you can trust. Your family is here for you. There's no place like home." Yet home was a miserable place filled with fighting and criticism, devoid of praise. Debby was rarely approved of, but her shortcomings were thrown up to her. Her father was a workaholic and usually unavailable. Her mother, a compulsive overeater and gambler, was away playing cards all day. Love was expressed either through excessive amounts of food or gifts of money.

Members of an overly clinging family feel as if they have no lives of their own. There is little or no privacy. John Bradshaw's description is that it is like being in a room with the doorknob on the outside. Anyone can invade your space any time, and there's nothing you can do about it. In a healthy family, it is like being in a room with the doorknob on the inside. You have control over your privacy, who you reveal your feelings and thoughts to, and the degree of intimacy you allow. Enmeshed families believe that your business is everybody's business. They feel free to criticize you even if you haven't asked for their views. There are few boundaries and no secrets. Nothing can be withheld.

You don't get to have a life of your own in this so-called loving family. The result is that you become an adult who believes that you are responsible for other people's happiness. You may look grown-up and live apart from them, but you can still be bound by an umbilical cord of guilt and shame.

COOL AND CALM

The distant family is characterized by a lack of emotion and few displays of affection. People don't act loving. They may be physically undemonstrative—rarely hugging, kissing or touching—and they also may withhold verbal expressions of warmth and support. Cool families may pressure members to overachieve, while at the same time being critical and perfectionistic.

I came from an emotionally cold family where achievement was prized. Although I brought home A's on my report card my parents rarely praised me. They just took it for granted. So I tried even harder to get a response. I graduated in the top ten percent of my high school class and was accepted by a prestigious college where I also excelled. I knew that my mother bragged about me to her friends and relatives, but she never told me that she was proud of me. How much would I have to do, how many honors would I have to earn to hear, "I love you?" I learned to reward myself by buying special gifts or sweets, and over the years developed these cravings into compulsions.

Distant families aren't even aware that they avoid emotion. They don't express anger openly or talk about their feelings. They just go through the motions. Again, to the casual observer, they may appear as well-adjusted as an episode of *Leave It To Beaver*. On the surface they seem a happy, caring group, but underneath the calm surface, the family member is in great pain because there is no intimacy.

The main characteristic of a dysfunctional family is that feelings are denied. The child has no one, and nowhere to go to resolve the situations and problems in his life. While these intense feelings of fear, anger, powerlessness or depression remain it feels like a sore that never heals. As the child grows he has to create his own solutions, without help from older and wiser advisers. These solutions are usually ineffective.

Many children who have been physically or emotionally abused learn to "split off" their feelings. They learn as small children to block the pain by going away in their imaginations, since they are unable to flee physically. As they grow, they continue to create ways to "split off" whenever the pain of living becomes too much. Abusing pleasurable substances and exciting activities is a way to leave one's cares behind . . . for the moment.

When you grow up in an inadequate family environment you aren't prepared to deal with life. When you find yourself in a risky situation or relationship, you may be overwhelmed by feelings of pain or helplessness. The families of many compulsive spenders reveal a history of alcohol, drug, or food abuse. Members of their family frequently suffer from chronic depression. Mix a biological predisposition toward addictive cravings, an unhappy family atmosphere and a society that encourages us to feel good at any cost, and the result is unhappy people who cannot control their compulsive urges to spend and debt.

YOU LEARN IT AT HOME

Compulsive spending and debting is not a disease. It is not genetic. It is a set of learned behaviors. Where do you learn them? Mostly at home! We learn our attitudes and many behaviors from watching the way our caregivers deal with life.

Kit was twenty-three years old and close to bankruptcy. Her parents were on the verge of losing their house because of bad debts and her mother's compulsive spending. Kit's father often worked two or three jobs, but couldn't keep the family solvent. Kit was not their natural daughter; she was adopted. This was the only family she knew.

Kit's mother had convinced her to get a large loan to help her through college, but Kit couldn't manage the too-large monthly payments. She hadn't realized it then because she was surrounded by people who lived constantly in debt. Kit just assumed that she could "make it" just like her parents seemed to. Once Kit got out into the world and tried to support herself she discovered that she didn't know how to save or budget, and she was a compulsive spender, just like Mom. She rarely could hang on to the little money she made.

Gary always started a new job with high hopes. He rationalized that the new job and steady income meant that he could treat himself to a new car or better place to live. He immediately began to get into debt. Before long, the bill collectors were knocking at the door and the dunning phone calls began. Gary didn't mind being harassed, but his wife became very nervous and frightened. She had never before experienced this kind of lifestyle. Yet, for Gary, this was not upsetting. His father was a poor businessman, and sometimes couldn't pay his bills. Gary remembered that when he was growing up, his parents were pressured by creditors. This was a familiar way of life for him, and he unconsciously recreated it in his world.

MY FAMILY MADE ME DO IT

Take a few minutes now to think about your upbringing. Your family and community, historical period you were born into, your education, and your personal experiences have created many attitudes and beliefs that you take for granted. A belief is simply a self-confirming theory. Perhaps it is time to reconsider what motivates your spending and debting behavior.

1. What economic group did your family belong to?
2. Who was the main wage earner?
3. Did your mother work?
4. What kind of work did your grandparents do? Were they successful?
5. Did your parents invest or save?
6. Did your parents use credit cards or incur debt? How?
7. Did you get an allowance?
8. When did you get your first job?
9. As you grew up, how did you think your financial needs would be met when you were an adult?

This game is called "*Mom said . . . Dad said . . ..*" For each topic I suggest, think about the adults who had the most influence on you. You may remember what your caregivers told you, but they may not have said anything to you about money, saving, spending, charging, or debting. Think hard about their actions. The old adage, "Actions speak louder than words" is often the case. How did they use money? What was not actually said but implied by silence or body language? Answer as best you can.

- Making money
  Mom said . . .
  Dad said . . .

- Spending money
  Mom said . . .
  Dad said . . .

- Saving money
  Mom said . . .
  Dad said . . .

- Shopping
  Mom said . . .
  Dad said . . .

- Credit buying
  Mom said . . .
  Dad said . . .

- Mom said I would grow up
  to be . . .
  to do . . .
  to have . . .

- Dad said I would grow up
  to be . . .
  to do . . .
  to have . . .

Is there someone you were named after or who you were told was like you? Are you supposed to have a life like that person's? Is it supposed to be a comedy, a tragedy or something else?

The beliefs that you have adopted because of your childhood training and experiences I call *commands*. Over the years I have collected the following commands from people who have attended my classes and workshops.

- Rich people are happy and poor people are sad.
- Rich people are mean.
- Poor are the salt of the earth.
- Poor people work harder, but enjoy life just as much in their own way.
- People like us "make do."
- You must earn it to enjoy it.
- Men make the money.
- Women don't work for the money.
- Do you *really* need this?
- You can do anything in life . . . but work hard.
- You can't take care of yourself.
- If you have a nickel, spend a dime.
- If you don't spend a lot for it, it isn't worth much.
- Don't pay retail prices.
- Business is too risky. Work for someone else.
- Possessions define who you are.
- Enjoy work, but don't worry about money. You'll get married.
- Money defines your worth.

Sid was living a hand-to-mouth existence. He was barely eking out a living in a low-paying part-time job.

Compulsive Spending: A Nation in Denial

He found many excuses for not seeking a better job, but none of them made sense. He was hell-bent to stay poor and needy. After surveying his family scene, Sid discovered that he had received a strange command: "All you have to do is make a connection with someone who will then give you a break. You aren't supposed to do it yourself. Someone else will do it for you." This belief paralyzed Sid. He was totally unable to assert himself effectively in the business world although he was a smart and capable man. I call this kind of command a "curse."

What are the commands that you have been carrying out? Has your behavior helped you or hurt you? What would you like to do about that?

To gain control of your compulsive behaviors take the time to answer the questions I have posed. Compare your story with those of other members of your family and ask close friends to tell you about their commands. You will discover that there are other alternatives to how you believe.

You do not have to think badly of yourself because of your heredity or upbringing. You do not have to be a slave of your compulsions! I have created the *STOP-LOOK-LISTEN Plan* to teach you how to change your thoughts and beliefs and how to change your overspending or debting behaviors.

The past is past. Blaming your family is a waste of time. They did the best they could. Now is the time to begin to change your life. You are the only person entitled to be in charge of your life!

4

SHOP TILL YOU DROP: THE SPENDING BINGE

A shopping binge is an episode of uncontrolled spending. Emotional energy characterizes the experience. Shopping can be exciting. Nothing compares with the thrill of the sale and snatching up a wonderful bargain. Many compulsive shoppers rationalize that it is okay because they got something at a good price.

The word "binge" is most commonly associated with the act of overeating. I use "binge" to describe all the ways that people act out compulsively. A shopping spree is a binge. The dictionary definition of the word *binge* is: "A period of excessive indulgence; a spree." When we indulge, we tell ourselves that we shouldn't, but . . .. We get carried away by our impulses and act as if we have no control over our behavior. In reality, we do have control over our choices, but the feeling of being carried away is how we rationalize our irresponsible behavior.

Compulsive Spending: A Nation in Denial

It is interesting to see how spenders' excuses sound like dieters' excuses: I couldn't help myself. This will be the last time I do it. How often does an opportunity like this come along? It was on sale so it doesn't really count. I'll start saving tomorrow.

Dr. Stanton Peele compares compulsive behaviors with powerful drug experiences when he says, "They are all-encompassing, quick and powerful in onset, and they make people less aware of and less able to respond to outside stimuli, people, and activities . . .. Such experiences succeed in blocking out sensations of pain, discomfort, or other negative sensations."

Spending binges are very much like food binges. Compulsive people buy things they don't need the same way compulsive eaters eat when they aren't hungry. They often buy what they can't afford or buy more than they need, like six pairs of shoes or a sweater in every color available. Spenders also buy beyond their "hunger." In other words, they go to the store to buy a blouse but end instead with shoes, a purse and many other purchases. Self-debtors are like anorexics because they deny themselves things and make do with less.

Countless compulsive spenders don't even wear or use what they buy. Price tags are not removed. Some objects remain in the original bag, which is carelessly thrown to the back of the closet. Very few shopaholics think of returning their purchases after the heat of the binge has cooled.

Loretta concentrated her compulsive urges on "areas" of products or items. She would focus on linens or china for a year or two until she became bored. Then she would choose a new category as the outlet for her craving for "things." Because of her compulsion to collect, she had cabinets full of paper weights, Japanese netsukes, and other art objects that crowded her living room and dining room.

SPENDING AS A TEMPER TANTRUM

Most binges seem like temper tantrums. When a spender feels angry, resentful, thwarted, or enraged, she will usually go shopping to run away from these intense emotions. Sometimes the urge to splurge comes after a long period of deprivation and going without. It is like holding your breath for as long as you can and then letting go. Then, one is never enough.

Most compulsive spenders are nice, nonassertive people who stuff their anger or unhappiness down inside themselves. As they feel more and more unhappy, instead of dealing with their life problem, they get the urge to go shopping. A spending binge is an outward manifestation of inner pain or anger.

Compulsive eaters constantly berate themselves because of how much they ate. Shopaholics feel guilty about how much they spend. They criticize themselves for buying things they don't need, and for spending money they don't have. If you think like this you are missing the point! Stop looking at the things you have bought, and think about the way you feel when you just *have* to spend. The intensity of the urge to spend reflects the amount of painful emotion or rage you are hiding from yourself. Throughout this book I will refer to people who "spend at" others to punish them or to soothe hurt feelings.

FILLING THE EMPTY PIT

The forever empty void can never be filled by things. Compulsive spenders turn to shopping when their needs aren't being met. Strolling through a beautiful mall or immersing yourself in gorgeous shop-by-mail catalogues is simply another way to run away from painful wounds of the past.

Human beings have three basic emotional needs:

Identity . . . Who Am I?
Relationship . . . Am I Lovable?
Power . . . Am I in Charge of My Life?

Who Am I? is a question most compulsive people cannot answer. Instead of knowing themselves and asserting their wishes, many people who abuse money have been knuckling under to others' wishes most of their lives.

Caroline was made to believe that she was a burden to the family. She was so neglected that she didn't learn to read until, when she was nine, a kind teacher discovered it and tutored her after school.

Nobody cared about her. Caroline comforts herself with furniture and art. She needs to discover that she is a lovable and capable person with many talents and high intelligence.

The emotional need for relationship involves a variety of transactions, from family interaction as a parent, sibling, or spouse to friendship and job related activities. Relationship needs bring up issues of getting love, warmth, friendship, affirmation of self, sex, affection, and unconditional acceptance by others.

Norma Jean was a bulimic and a compulsive shopper. After her parents' divorce, she felt compelled to take care of her unhappy mother. Norma Jean became terrified if her mother seemed depressed. Since she couldn't burden her mother with her problems because she feared making her mother's depression worse, she would sometimes binge and sometimes splurge at the thrift store. Norma Jean told herself that people wouldn't like her if she seemed to have troubles. Therefore, she had nowhere to go with her intense feelings of unhappiness and fear. Her only outlets were food and shopping.

Power over one's life is an important issue for spenders. Part of their existence is a struggle between control and being controlled by others or by their "appetite."

Sibyl, the "Poor Little Rich Girl" I told you about earlier, thought of herself as the forgotten child. She was a girl in a family where girls were unimportant.

She discovered that the way to avoid the pain of being discounted was to hide in her bed. Today Sibyl uses her money, not to buy clothes and objects, but to go away to the mountains or rent a cabin in the wilderness where she can continue to hide.

When a spender tells me that she has been on a shopping spree and can't figure out why, I ask her two simple questions: (1) What is going on right now in your life that is upsetting? (2) Which of your needs is not being met?

THE BINGE CYCLE

The compulsive cycle, to which spenders so often return, can be broken down into a series of steps. Although the urge to spend or shop may seem to come out of the blue without reason, there is a pattern that is the same each time. The causes of the binge may vary, but the episode is made up of these steps:

1. Trigger
2. Desire/Decision
3. Action
4. Hangover
5. Letdown
6. Back where you began

The Trigger is a very powerful emotional feeling arising from a situation or relationship in your life. Some triggers are one-time experiences; others are daily happenings. The most common feelings that shoppers try to avoid are: anger, loneliness, rejection, resentment, helplessness, depression, and boredom. These feelings may originate at home or at work. Your reaction to the time-of-year and what is going on in the world also can contribute to your decision to splurge. Most important are your everyday feeling arising from meaningful personal and professional relationships, or lack of them.

The trigger leads to the *Desire/Decision*. Every consumer has moments when she thinks about going shopping. Sometimes she goes, and sometimes she decides not to go. For compulsive spenders there is only one thought, "I want it—I'll have it." The desire and the decision are merged.

Action follows the decision. Each compulsive spender observes his or her personal ritual around money. Some only shop at thrift stores, others love sales. Some compulsive spenders have a hobby or collection that takes them to auctions or special sales. Couch potatoes can binge in front of the TV with shopping programs, a telephone, and a credit card.

The aftereffect is called the *Hangover*. The hangover can occur right after the shopping expedition or later when the shopper receives the bill in the mail. Feelings of guilt, shame, self-hatred, hopelessness, helplessness, or depression arise. The shopper promises herself that she will stop, try harder to live within her means, or never debt again.

But after all is said and done, the *Letdown* washes over her. Nothing has been accomplished by splurging. Nothing has changed. She feels more unhappy than ever, and now she is deeper in debt. She is now *back to where she began*. The situation or relationship she is in pain about is still the same.

We all experience good times and bad times. Most people can cope with the added stress brought on by illness, loss, disappointment, rejection, and loneliness. The spectrum of well-being and unhappiness you can live with, without becoming ill physically or emotionally, is your *emotional comfort zone*.

Let us imagine that a well-adjusted person has a comfort zone of plus 50 to minus 50. People who are less able to cope with life stress, like many compulsive spenders and debtors, may have a comfort zone of only plus 20 to minus 20. I have treated some with an even narrower limit—plus 10 to minus 10—and who therefore always feel overwhelmed by life. When compulsive spenders find themselves in discomfort extending beyond their comfort zone, they often attempt to stop the pain or distract themselves from it by spending.

Certain individuals are set off after being with a specific person, a parent, sibling or authority figure. Some situations that trigger a binge occur every day. Gail hated housework and child care. Shopping was a way to leave the house and to cheer herself up. The things she bought were a reward for all the hard work she did that her husband didn't appreciate.

WHAT CREATES URGES AND CRAVINGS?

The desire to go shopping or spend money you don't have by using credit is not a mystical happening. There are several common factors that create over-spending: conditioning, environmental cues, beliefs, emotional discomfort, and dependency or withdrawal from other addictive substances or behaviors.

Conditioning is the automatic way you react with money. Evelyn was brought up in an extremely wealthy home, but now that she was an adult she earned very little. Even so, she shopped in elegant boutiques and continued to act rich. For her parents' anniversary she spent almost one thousand dollars for a gift, although her salary was about eight dollars per hour.

Environmental cues are the ways you react to your surroundings. Going to a mall or swap meet is an environmental cue. Shops to spend in are there. Christmas or birthdays are for buying presents. Jack considered his paycheck to be an environmental stimulus. His paycheck represented money, and money is for spending. Jack complained, "If I don't see it, I won't spend it."

Beliefs are like commands that we follow without evaluating or questioning. When Loretta, the collector, saw a piece of china that she craved, she rationalized that it was okay to spend her money because her husband was there to take care of the family. Kit maintained that God would provide, therefore she didn't have to save money out of her paycheck. Dave, the "Rebel," was a big spender, treating people and giving gifts. His belief was that he was a generous person, and that is how generous people act.

I have already explained that spending and debting are the ways many unhappy people medicate emotional pain. When you find yourself in a high-risk situation and cannot cope, the result is misery. Since you don't know how to handle yourself, you must resort to the only ways you know to feel more comfortable. Often those ways are to abuse substances or pleasurable activities.

Most compulsive spenders and debtors I have known are people with more than one compulsion. Loretta's compulsive urges to collect art only became evident to me while we were working on her compulsive eating disorder. Many of my clients are practicing a Twelve-Step program in Alcoholics Anonymous, Overeaters Anonymous, or similar programs. As they give up one addictive substance, they are often unaware of the subtle way that they begin to use money compulsively. Gail and Gary were both abstinent in Overeaters Anonymous. Although they were no longer food binge buddies, they continued to binge with their credit cards and spent hours pouring over the Sears catalogue together. Kit was free from binge/purges but began to haunt the mall whenever she had a fight with her boyfriend.

YOU CAN LEARN FROM YOUR BEHAVIOR

Although this book is meant to help you eliminate spending binges and irresponsible debting, these behaviors may not go away overnight. Instead of hating yourself, start by doing a postmortem on the unwelcome behaviors you are still plagued by.

Remind yourself of the factors that create urges and cravings to spend. Are you setting yourself up by allowing yourself to be in environments, social situations or relationships you can't handle? Are you so intent on giving up one type of addiction that you are still in denial about your spending or debting? Next, are you willing to ask yourself what feelings you might be avoiding or what situations or relationships are producing anxiety?

Like most compulsive shoppers, Kit wanted to berate herself for her latest shopping binge. Instead I insisted that she could learn something valuable from her behavior. What feeling or event triggered her binge? Kit was working hard for a promotion at work. Another woman was competing with her and trying to undermine her success. Kit was angry with her competitor and angry that her boss wasn't willing to side with her against the other woman. Also, Kit was afraid that maybe she wasn't as qualified as she wanted people to think she was. Her inability to express her feelings to her boss for fear of appearing unprofessional caused extreme anxiety. Part of her rationale for shopping was to buy clothes that would enhance her business wardrobe (make her look good on the outside while she silently worried on the inside).

Once Kit realized that she made herself feel powerless by not asking for what she wanted and second guessing her supervisor's thoughts, she began to feel as if she had more control over her work situation. Compulsive spenders like Kit need to recognize the feelings that trigger a spree and learn how to handle them without denial or avoidance.

CAN COMPULSIVE SPENDING BE GOOD?

If you are like most compulsive spenders, you constantly tell yourself that you are bad. Did it ever occur to you that a shopping spree could be good? A binge may be a new opportunity for learning. A client of mine said, "Failure is the opportunity to begin again more intelligently." A headache is sometimes a signal of stress. A desire to spend or debt is also a signal of stress. Most people are quick to listen to physical pain and go to the doctor. Compulsive people have difficulty accepting a binge as a signal of emotional pain and, instead of taking healing action, they cover it over with the pleasure of shopping or spending.

I have warning lights on the dashboard of my car. If there is a dangerously low level of oil, a red light goes on. A spending binge is like that red light. The binge behavior is telling you that you are feeling a "dangerous" level of DIS-EASE. You are neither a good nor a bad person for giving in to the overwhelming urge to spend. You are a person in pain who is ignoring the pain. The pain will not go away unless you get to its source.

A desire to spend is a reminder of a problem you are not heeding. In order to be freed of your compulsion you will have to become aware of your feelings, and you will have to modify or change your behavior around money. Every binge makes a statement. In this book I will teach you to decode the message of your compulsive acts and create new tools for solving life's problems.

As you read you will learn about the *STOP-LOOK-LISTEN Plan* to help you change your behavior and control the situations and relationships in your life that create unhappiness and lead to spending.

A SELF-HELP PROGRAM
FOR CHANGE

5

THE STOP–LOOK–LISTEN PLAN: AN OVERVIEW

The problem of compulsive spending and debting can be overcome permanently if you take action. The *STOP—LOOK—LISTEN Plan* is a multidimensional one that teaches you to make changes on the behavioral level, the emotional level, the intellectual or thinking level, and the inner-power level. I once thought that behavior modification alone was all that was needed to overcome compulsive behaviors. Yet self-awareness isn't enough. I have received many phone calls from people who each say the same thing: "I know why I'm doing it, but I can't stop. What's wrong with me? I'm an intelligent, capable person yet I act stupid when it comes to spending."

Many people can go along under control for months or years, but when there is a life crisis or significant change, they will revert to old behaviors. Wanda had carefully saved $5,000 to redecorate her living room. Her mother died suddenly, and Wanda was overwhelmed with grief. She wanted understanding and support from her husband during this mourning period, but he acted cold and distant. Wanda wasn't consciously aware of how hurt and sad she felt. All she realized was that she "frittered away" the $5,000 on nothing and was left with no resources to redo her living room.

Some compulsive spenders have been in conventional psychotherapy and never mentioned their spending or debting problem to the therapist. Sometimes these people do experience improvement with other issues in their lives because of psychotherapy, but the compulsive behavior doesn't change. I have spoken with therapists who simply don't recognize the importance of dealing with compulsive spending behaviors as a key to understanding emotional upheavals in their client's life. Often they just ignore the evidence or deal with it superficially.

Since most compulsive spenders aren't conscious of the connection between emotions and behavior, they have to work backward from the overt behavior, the spending spree, to the root cause: the spender's thought system. The *STOP—LOOK—LISTEN Plan* teaches spenders to acknowledge their behavior and become willing to understand their misuse of money without negative self-judgment, to look for the intense feelings that trigger the behavior, to reach for the underlying thoughts and beliefs that give rise to those feelings, and to take action to avoid further anxiety and subsequent compulsive episodes.

Psychologists have discovered that addictive and compulsive behaviors can be eliminated when people feel as if they can control the outcomes in life that matter to them. We call this quality "self-efficacy." If you think you can't change, you can't. The more you can control the outcome of the situations of your life, the less you will give in to urges and cravings to spend unwisely.

Compulsive actions will continue unless you understand how you create them, and will end only when you develop new skills to deal with life. Four important factors that lead to compulsive behaviors with money are: (1) inability to fulfill your emotional needs; (2) values that support irresponsible compulsive behavior; (3) lack of self restraint; and (4) feelings of powerlessness over your life or your compulsion.

Compulsive spenders seek experiences that satisfy needs they cannot seem to fulfill any other way. There are always three components of the compulsive act: (1) the person; (2) the situation or environment; and (3) the experience. I have created the *STOP—LOOK— LISTEN Plan* to enable compulsive money abusers to demystify the problem and take positive charge.

This is how I work with a client. Step one is an examination of her spending diary. The spending diary shows how much she spent, what she spent it on, and when and where. She also must note times that she had the urge to shop though she resisted it successfully.

Step two is to examine each urge or binge and look for the feelings that particular binge was camouflaging. For instance, one client had a disagreement with her business partner. She was driving home, still angry because she had given in to his demands. As she passed a large department store complex, she found herself pulling into the parking lot. She proceeded to shop and bought six sweaters that she neither needed nor could afford. This woman was having a temper tantrum. She still felt angry with her partner but also felt powerless because he had won.

Behind every binge is an intense emotion—either positive or negative—that is uncomfortable. It may take a little practice to learn to uncover that emotion and the situation or relationship from which it arose. That is why I also ask people to note the urges that they resisted. Every urge reflects a potentially difficult situation or intense emotion.

The third step is to go beyond the emotion and the experience that created it to the thought or idea that caused that particular feeling. My client's anger at her partner arose from these thoughts:

- My partner didn't listen to my ideas. He had his mind made up that he was right.
- My partner didn't respect me enough to discuss things. He told me what to do as if I were a child and he was my father.
- Maybe I'm not smart enough to be in my own business.
- My partner is also my boyfriend. If I disagree with him, maybe he'll leave me.

In step three I work with my clients to recognize how their thoughts or beliefs may not be the truth, although they feel true. We go over each thought or belief and rewrite it in another more positive way. Once this compulsive spender could accept that she was an equal partner in the business and was both intelligent and entitled to be listened to, she could handle disagreements with her partner in a new way that enabled her to feel okay and stop spending at him.

STEP ONE IS TO STOP AND TAKE STOCK

All compulsive spenders want to be free of their loss of control around shopping and spending. They want desperately to eliminate the binge behavior. The belief that when the symptom goes away they are cured is not so. Unless there are changes in lifestyle, belief systems, and problem-solving skills, the compulsion may return during times of anxiety and stress.

Before spenders can start on a daily program for change, they must know who they are financially. First, take stock of your financial status. List all your assets. Next list all your liabilities: credit card debt, loans and mortgages, personal debts. Finally, make a chart of your weekly or monthly expenses: rent, phone, utilities, gasoline, food, medical, and all other obligations.

Once you know what you have and what you need to live, you will have a clearer idea of your financial life. Now you are ready to begin your daily expense diary. Keeping track every day is essential to achieve a sense of awareness of your behavior, and it will help you take responsibility for your choices. Taking stock daily will provide you with the written record that graphs your emotional ups and downs.

Changing your behavior and eliminating cravings and urges to spend involves making new choices about what to buy and how much to spend. You will need to develop new ways of thinking and feeling about money and credit. As you begin to write down everything you spend, you will experience new feelings that may surprise you.

STEP TWO IS TO LOOK AT YOUR EMOTIONS

A binge is a cover-up and tells you that you are not being honest with yourself about your feelings or the intensity of your emotions. You may be denying negative emotions such as anger, guilt, fear, shame, and hurt. Perhaps you are trying to talk yourself out of your resentment through self-discount, a process in which you don't give yourself permission to feel anything negative because you believe that it is bad or people won't like you. The result of self-discount is that you keep yourself a victim, continue to feel helpless, and rage at your helplessness.

Start by accepting the idea that the urge to spend is an explosion of emotion. Then practice being in touch with feelings, knowing what feelings are, and relating feelings to situations or relationships. By postponing the onset of the shopping binge, you can get in touch with the feeling that drives you to distract yourself by spending. When you can interrupt the compulsive cycle, you are on the road to recovery.

Before Connie was married she overspent on gourmet foods and lived like a princess. After her marriage she still sought food. Connie found that she often felt as if she had to make a quick trip to the market for some milk or bread. Although she didn't overspend when she went, she realized that her quick-fix market trips were ways of running away from home when she was annoyed with her husband. Once she began to resist the urge, she had to free the feelings of anger or resentment. She then decided to learn how to express her feelings and communicate them with her husband instead of shopping to avoid her anger. Soon both of them felt much happier because Connie could bring her resentments out in the open and find ways to resolve the couple's problems.

I have worked with some individuals who have had previous psychotherapy and can tune in to their emotions with ease. Some of these people are stuck in the feeling state and act as if feelings were facts. Thus, intense fear or guilt will paralyze them as they tell themselves, "Something terrible will happen" or "It's all my fault." Often feelings are a result of your fantasies or fears and are not the truth. To free yourself from being a slave to feelings, you must practice the next step: *listen.*

STEP THREE IS TO LISTEN TO YOUR SELF-TALK

I described Dave earlier as having a "hole in his pocket" and wanting to live affluently. Dave had two closets full of clothing. One Saturday he found himself wanting to go shopping for a new sport jacket. The urge was very strong. Dave decided to postpone the binge while he examined what was going on. He knew that the new jacket was for a party he was going to that night. What was he thinking about the coming event? "Will I be accepted tonight? Will I have a good time? I have a better chance of meeting a woman if I look good. I'd better get a new jacket so I'll be sure to look perfect." Dave's thoughts reinforced an underlying sense of inadequacy. His fears of not being attractive or good enough plus his loneliness for a new relationship were the real issues, not buying new clothes.

Dave could substitute positive alternatives such as:

- I can have a good time if I decide to, no matter what I wear.
- I have many good-looking jackets already. I can look good wearing one of them.
- I don't have to look perfect to be accepted.
- Women can like me because of my intelligence, friendliness and sense of humor, not because of my jacket.

Your thoughts and beliefs influence your feelings. It is common in Twelve-Step groups for members to introduce themselves by saying, "I'm Jane, an alcoholic (or compulsive overeater, gambler, etc.)" Mary pondered the outcome of constantly labeling herself as a person with a lifetime problem. She decided to change her greeting to, "Hello, I'm Mary, a committed abstainer." Instead of dwelling on the negative, Mary allied herself with her commitment to abstain from compulsive behavior. By affirming her goal to stop acting out and be in charge of her behavior, she accepted her power and chose to be responsible. Give yourself new watchwords and self descriptions, and you will feel different and act differently.

Understanding the interrelationship between your behavior, feelings, and thoughts will lead to dramatic change. By practicing awareness techniques and skills in listening to your inner dialogue and changing it, you can be your own therapist.

TAKE ACTION

You have the power to take action. There are many undiscovered capacities within you just below the surface of your awareness. You are more than you think you are. As you learn to undo your negative self-talk, you will find yourself ready and able to behave in a new and healthy way.

Remember the three A's: AWARENESS, ACCEPTANCE and ACTION! Awareness means being willing to feel your feelings and name them. Acceptance means that you stop feeling stupid or childish for having these feeling. Stop justifying them. You may not want to feel afraid, powerless, angry, or guilty, but you do.

A Self-Help Program for Change

You cannot change anything until you accept your situation. Only then can you take action to resolve the problems caused by unhappy situations or relationships.

A most important tool for change is the power of faith or spiritual belief. For those who use prayer or meditation, this practice will help you employ your spirituality to change your behavior. Relying on a Higher Power, as in the Twelve-Step programs, brings dramatic results for many. Some individuals like to read uplifting books, attend church, or learn how to meditate.

There is a creative unconscious within each human being that can be used as an ally to aid you in your search for happiness. You can learn to get in touch with this special inner self through journal writing, guided imagery, art, music and even dream interpretation. Exploring the spiritual or transpersonal realm may be a new and wonderful adventure for a person who is caught up in the belief that he has an insurmountable problem.

In the final analysis, what works best is a combination of these elements:

- Develop a strong desire to change.
- Learn to recognize, accept and cope with negative feelings and experiences.
- Develop new inner and outer resources for change.
- Learn how to control stress and fear.

- Reevaluate your values in terms of the negative effects of spending and debting.

The best thing you can do is to learn how to control your destiny and work toward a goal of rewarding work and relationships. The STOP-LOOK-LISTEN program will help compulsive spenders and debtors to understand the dynamics of their behavior and to make changes necessary for permanent recovery. The program I have created is simple. Here are the steps to follow:

STOP: Evaluate your compulsive behaviors and your urges to spend. Rate each episode on a scale of 1 to 10 (with 10 being the most intense).

LOOK: Name the feelings that triggered your compulsive acts. What specific situation or relationship is involved?

LISTEN: Write down your self-talk about this situation or relationship. Examine your negative self-talk. Rewrite it in a positive way. Decide what action is appropriate to change the troublesome situation or relationship.

6

STOP
AND CHANGE WHAT YOU DO

If you sweep your spending binges or debting behaviors under the rug of your unconsciousness with rationalizations and denial, you will never learn to stop. The hardest part of changing your behavior is to decide to become aware of it and accept responsibility for it.

The first part of the three-step recovery program is called STOP. I know that if you could stop your self-defeating behaviors you would. You are reading this book because you haven't been able to stop and stay stopped. STOP means to stop right now and take stock. It means to commit yourself to begin to make conscious choices, to recognize when you have succumbed to compulsion and stop rationalizing or making excuses. And STOP means to take concrete and specific actions that I will describe in this chapter.

A Self-Help Program for Change

EXAMINE YOUR FINANCIAL STATE

Begin by collecting information about your behavior with money and credit. Take out your checkbook, payroll stubs, receipts, and bills for the last year. It is time to examine your expenses and cash flow. First look at what comes in each month. Add up your earnings, child support received, benefits, and any other source of income. Make note of any savings, stocks or bonds, investments, property or other assets.

Now turn to your outflow. Start with the large fixed monthly expenses such as rent or mortgage payments, car payments, loan payments, and alimony or child support. If taxes are not deducted from your paycheck, list how much you pay in federal, state, and local taxes and social security. Other regular expenses may include life insurance, health insurance, car insurance, and home or renter's insurance premiums.

Household and personal payments such as telephone bills, gas, electricity, water, garbage, and credit card payments are also monthly obligations. Don't forget medical or dental bills, payments on TV, furniture, or other big-ticket purchases. How much do you spend on food each month, grocery shopping and eating out? Child care, baby-sitting, and school tuition must be included in your list.

Less regular but equally important expenses are those for your car: gasoline, maintenance, parking, license or registration. If you have no car, include the cost of using other transportation. Other common expenses include: spending for cigarettes, entertainment, recreation, vacations, club or organization dues, housecleaning, laundry and dry cleaning, newspapers or magazine subscriptions, pet care, haircuts and beauty parlor expenses, donations to charity, and childrens' allowances.

Finally, add up your total yearly income and your total yearly expenses. What is the status of your financial health? What do you want to do about it? The first step is to stop incurring more debt. This is done by keeping track of what you spend each day. As you note the amounts you spend and what you spend it on, you may want to add thoughts about your feelings too.

THE EXPENSE DIARY

The expense diary is the central tool for the beginning of self-awareness. If you write down what you spend, you will know what you are doing. If you don't, you will perpetuate delusions and denial. To write down the numbers late at night or after a week has passed is a waste of time. You need to pay as you go. The expense diary is not a report card! It is not a paper that reveals whether you are good or bad. It is the raw data of your life. You can't solve your problem unless you have the facts to work from. The expense diary is like a graph. It will reflect what is going on in your life day-by-day.

Some people only want to write down the "good" days. You will learn more from the "bad" days than the "good" ones. Once you get past your reluctance to look at what you are doing, you have made headway.

Whether you choose a small notebook or a piece of paper, WRITE DOWN WHAT YOU SPEND! What do you do if you record for a day or two and then skip and feel so guilty that you don't go back to the diary because you "blew it" by overspending or skipping days? Start by asking yourself a few simple questions that will help you make a commitment to yourself that is loving and reasonable:

- Am I willing to keep an expense diary?
- What kind of record keeping am I willing to do? Am I willing to write down the amount and what I purchased? Am I willing to write about my feelings too?
- How many days will I *really* keep my promise to keep an expense diary?

Please be aware that you may be asking yourself how many days the experts expect you to write your expenditures . . . seven days every week. That is not what I asked though. My questions is: In your heart of hearts, how many days will you actually do it?

Begin where you are, not where you think you should be or where others think you should be. If you write down four days' worth of spending a week, but sternly mandate seven days, you will feel like a loser. Go over the questions again. Be brutally honest with yourself. You may be willing to write down only one day this week. WONDERFUL! Now do it!

Each week make a new commitment. Accept yourself as you are today, and let yourself do a less-than-perfect job so long as you make a beginning. Perhaps next week you will commit yourself to only one day again, but the following week you may know you can handle three days. Write what you are willing to keep track of, but keep writing.

It is difficult for a compulsive spender to read his or her expense diary objectively. You may tend to judge yourself as bad when you binge or overspend. The expense diary has vital information for you. Perhaps you have a friend you can trust enough to share your record. If you have a therapist or Twelve-Step sponsor, they will surely be willing to help you. See if you can reread your diary with new eyes. Here are some questions that may help you:

1. How much money did you spend each day this week?
2. Is each day the same in pattern and amount spent? Which days are different? How are they different? What was happening on the days you spent out of control?
3. Are weekends different from weekdays? What are the differences?
4. Were there any days or times of day that were more stressful to you? Was this feeling the same every day or did it occur just occasionally during the week?
5. Did you feel upset or anxious about any people in your life? What days did this occur? Look at

your spending for that day or the next. Did it reflect these feelings?

6. Did you try to stay on a strict money diet, and deprive yourself, or did you allow yourself to spend a moderate amount for pleasure? Did you feel powerful and in control? Did you feel scared? Did it lead to a binge?

7. Looking over your entire weekly diary, what did you learn?

THE BINGE RATING SYSTEM

The expense diary will show you when you are spending emotionally. Many compulsive spenders can't tune in to the intensity of their feelings. I have, therefore, devised a system to help you learn how to link your spending behavior to the experiences of your life. I call it the *Binge Rating System*.

Here is what you do. Most people have heard of the Richter scale, which measures earthquakes on a scale of 1 to 10. Some tremors register 4.5; others, 6.8 or 8.2.

1. Read over your expense diary in the evening. Look for episodes of compulsive spending or intense urges to spend.

2. Rate each as if it were a quake. Use the scale of 1 to 10. The higher number does not reflect the amount of money you spent but the intensity of the URGE to spend.

3. Ask yourself what happened in the last twenty-four hours that upset you that intensely.

Rating your spending by its intensity rather than the amount spent may enable you to understand yourself better. Each compulsive spender must have the freedom to evaluate his performance. Toni, the "Second Hand Rose," splurged at thrift stores while Loretta bought works of art worth thousands. It was not how much they spent but their uncontrollable need to spend that is the key.

Even if you are resistant to keeping a daily diary you may find that rating your spending behavior each evening can be an interesting and useful habit. Plan a few minutes of daily review in which you ask yourself three easy questions:

Daily Review

1. Today, how do I rate my urges to overspend on an emotional earthquake scale of 1 to 10?
2. What was the emotional equivalent of that rating in terms of situations and relationships in my life?
3. How can I do something to change the situation I am reacting to?

AVOID DEPRIVATION

In my work with compulsive eaters and bulimics, I often shock my clients when I insist that they learn how to stop dieting. A diet is temporary deprivation to prepare for eating again. The columnist Art Buchwald once said that the word "diet" comes from the verb "to die." I insist that my clients allow themselves to eat a moderate amount of something they love every day. They know that they will have something good tomorrow and tomorrow and tomorrow. It immediately cuts down the number of food binges they have. No one likes to feel deprived. No matter how hard we try to martyr ourselves, somewhere along the line we are tempted to forget the whole plan and indulge.

Jerrold Mundis suggests the same approach in his book *How to Get Out of Debt, Stay Out of Debt and Live Prosperously*. He talks about a budget the way I counsel people about diets. After all, a budget is simply a money diet. He writes, "A sense of insufficiency and restriction is inherent in the word, a sense of not having enough. A budget confines you to a dark little room while everyone else is outside playing in the sunlight."

An important suggestion he makes is that no matter how much you are in debt, you must continue to spend money on yourself for entertainment or to feel good. If you don't, you are likely to splurge with a spending spree.

I tell my food addicts that when they eat what they want the most, it is easy to say no to other urges. This is true of money too. Instead of buying everything or five of a kind, think about what you REALLY want most. Is what you want to buy worth it TO YOU?

Connie earned lots of money and liked fine things, but her overspending was mainly around food, gourmet items, five-of-a-kind, and eating in very expensive restaurants. When you stop trying to "diet" with money and learn to become conscious by keeping a daily record, you will begin to behave more responsibly with your money. Every time you have to write something down, it enables you to pause and rethink your choice. Here is a handy technique I call the Five W's. Use it when you are in doubt about your decision to spend.

- What's going on?
- What do I feel? (mad, glad, sad, scared)
- What do I want to do?
- What will be the consequence?
- What do I choose to do?

This exercise may not automatically stop you from spending, but it will enhance your consciousness of your behavior and help you to change.

HANDLING TEMPTATION

Temptation often arises from environmental cues. Where you are, and with whom, may trigger a spending spree. When they had nothing to do, Gail and Gary would walk around the mall to window-shop. Although this couple had little money to spend, they invariably ended up going into a store and charging things. They rationalized by agreeing that what they bought was for the house, something they really needed, like a new broom or tool. Nevertheless, they were increasing their debt.

Gail and Gary were binge-buddies. They egged each other on and kept each other from feeling guilty over their spending sprees. Do you have someone who is a binge-buddy? Someone you shop with or talk about shopping with? Perhaps you need to rethink your relationship now.

Shops and malls are instant temptation for compulsive shoppers. So are some kinds of vacations. Free ports are offering bargains. Certain countries are known for specialty items. Craft fairs and swap meets are places to spend. Think about how you like to spend your time. Can you begin to plan experiences that are not involved with opportunities to spend money or shop? Take a walk in nature or play a sport. Read a book or take time for an enjoyable hobby.

Another married couple, Josie and Mark, were also binge-buddies but they spent money on expensive vacations and time-sharing condos. As the balance of their credit cards climbed, they decided to consolidate their debt by taking on a loan to pay off all their existing loans. You cannot get out of debt by borrowing more money! Within a short time they began to build up their Visa and Mastercards again, only now they also had the consolidation loan payment to consider.

Compulsive spenders and debtors do best when they cut up their credit cards and learn to live on cash. Neither Gail and Gary nor Josie and Mark knew how to do this. Gail and Gary hired a financial guide to help them pay off their existing debt and live within their means. He helped them create a payback plan and gave them a weekly allowance. Members of Debtors Anonymous can find similar help within that program. Some people enlist the aid of an accountant or other financial professional. If you don't know what to do, ask for help.

MALL THERAPY

This technique is one you can do yourself to promote immediate changes in your behavior. You will need the aid of someone you can trust to carry out this experiment. Make sure the person you choose is free from compulsive spending problems.

Explain to your companion that you are performing an experiment to find out more about yourself. The other person needs to promise to be supportive and not make any judgmental comments. Pick a shopping mall or area, even a large department store is fine. You can decide to go during a slow time or a very busy Saturday. Plan to stay for one hour. Here is a list of questions that you can have your helper ask you as you progress through the hour:

1. After you enter the mall or store, look around and take stock of the situation. Ask yourself how anxious, fearful, or excited you are on a scale of 1 to 10. Talk about your feelings. What are you telling yourself?

2. Find the mall or store directory and read it through quickly. What are your thoughts? Which shops or departments are the hardest to resist? Which are the easiest? Share your feelings with your helper and select a destination.

3. As you walk toward your destination become aware of your reactions to the other areas you pass. How do you feel? What tempting thoughts might you be experiencing? It is okay to window shop. Keep verbalizing your feelings and thoughts as you do.

4. When you reach your destination, stop for a moment and rate your anxiety on the 1 to 10 scale. What are you telling yourself about this place? What do you want to do? What will happen if you do? Is this okay? Do you want to act in a new way? Share your thoughts with your companion as you browse or try on things. How do you feel? What do you want to do now? What do you do?

5. Leave the store and find a place to stop and take stock. How do you feel about the choices you made? Did your actions help you or hurt you? Would you act differently next time?

6. Ask your friend what he or she thought about as you both walked around and looked at stores or merchandise. Does this person think the way you do? Compare your ideas with each other. If your friend's outlook is different, try not to

think of it as a criticism. What have you learned?

7. If there is time, pick a second shop. Go through the same steps, 4, 5, 6. See if anything has changed.

8. Leave the mall or the store. How do you feel right now? Are you anxious, guilty, elated? Rate your emotional level. What have you just learned? What changes can you put into action immediately?

One helpful plan is to make a promise to shop only with a list. Stay aware of the temptations of the stores or windows "calling to you." Pretend that you are wearing blinders. Another hint is to set a specific time allotment for your shopping excursion, just enough time to get the things on your list. Become accountable for leaving the store at the promised time, no matter what.

The exercise I have just described also can be done in front of your TV as you watch a home-shopping program, if this is one of your compulsions. Make sure you have a helper take you through the questions as the program progresses.

Reading about how to change can be informative, but actually to do it is sometimes difficult. When you find yourself resisting change, you may begin to hate yourself and may quit without giving yourself enough time to find ways to overcome your resistance. Working with a therapist or support group can help you to push past the stumbling block and learn to confront your conflicts and fears. The important thing is to dedicate yourself to the idea that you can overcome your spending or debting problem, no matter what it takes.

7

LOOK
AT YOUR EMOTIONAL LIFE

Most compulsive spenders haven't a hint of what has triggered the urge to spend. Perhaps later they realize that something has upset them, or perhaps it is buried too quickly and too deep. But it is there below the surface. With some careful questioning the feelings will emerge.

An example is what happened to Lupe. Lupe and her friend Wendy were going to get together after Lupe's dental appointment. Wendy lived nearby. That morning, when Lupe called to confirm their date, Wendy said she couldn't make it until an hour later. Lupe was stuck with time on her hands. A park and a shopping mall were nearby. Lupe, the compulsive clothing buyer, chose the mall and made a dent in her charge cards.

Later Lupe was remorseful and angry with herself for splurging. She didn't know what had set her off. She hadn't intended to go shopping. I asked her how she felt when Wendy changed their plans. Lupe felt disappointed, angry, and frustrated. Apparently, Wendy often did this—changed plans at the last moment. Lupe's spending binge was a temper tantrum. She was angry at being "jerked around" by Wendy once too often, but she hadn't realized how upset she had actually been.

WHAT ARE FEELINGS?

A common error in our culture is that we say "think" when we should say "feel" and say "feel" when we should say "think." "I *feel* that you don't like me" and "I *feel* that I should stop shopping" are two cases in point. If you don't know the difference between a feeling and a thought, you will have trouble understanding how you create a binge. In each sentence the word *think* should be substituted for the word *feel*: "I *think* you don't like me" and "I *think* that I should stop shopping."

Feel refers to a feeling, a sensation or emotion, not a thought. What comes after the word feel ought to be the name of a feeling: "I feel *angry* when you don't call to say you will be late" or "I feel *scared* when I sing in public."

Use the word think when you say *that*. Remember the original mistaken sentences: "I feel *that* you don't like me" and "I feel *that* I should stop shopping." When you use the word *that* to explain, you are really referring to a thought you are thinking and not to a feeling you are experiencing. Can you see the way to use these two words in the following examples?

"I *feel angry* when you don't call to say you will be late because I *think that* you don't care about me."

"I *think that* I should stop shopping because I *feel overwhelmed* by the stores at the mall."

"I *think that* you don't like me because you frowned at me just now and I *felt uncomfortable*."

We can divide the range of human emotions into four basic classifications: mad, glad, sad, and scared. Here is a list of variations you may want to refer to.

MAD: resentful, irritated, furious, annoyed, offended, irate, frustrated, fuming, boiling, indignant, cross, bitter, enraged, hateful, disinterested

GLAD: happy, satisfied, serene, comfortable, joyous, pleased, ecstatic, excited, exhilarated, thrilled, relaxed, enthusiastic, cheery, lighthearted, proud, warm

SAD: unhappy, depressed, gloomy, ashamed, discouraged, dismal, heavyhearted, disappointed, in-the-dumps, blah, melancholy, sullen, discontented, embarrassed, useless

SCARED: afraid, timid, panicky, alarmed, insecure, nervous, anxious, worried, dismayed, threatened, petrified, shaky, terrified, cautious, frightened, mixed-up, uptight, abandoned

A Self-Help Program for Change

These are only a few samples of the many words that can help you become more sensitive to what is happening inside you. If you have trouble tuning in to what you are feeling, start by asking yourself the basic four: Am I mad, glad, sad, or scared?

Beware of the "umbrella words!" An umbrella word is a common word that is too general in meaning. "Nervous," "good," and "bad" are three umbrella words. "Nervous" can mean scared, angry, sad, or frustrated, depending on who is speaking. Eliminate these three words from your vocabulary and replace them with more precise words to describe your emotions and you will get a clearer picture of the feeling that triggers your urges to spend.

Here is a simple exercise to practice naming your feelings. Take a piece of paper and complete the following sentence ten to twenty times. You may want to address each sentence to a different person or just one individual. Be sure to include both positive and negative feelings from the above list.

I feel _____ when you _____ because I am telling myself that _____.

"Telling myself" is the same as thinking. It may come out like this: John, I feel happy when you call me up during the day from work because I think that you care about me and enjoy making contact.

John, I feel ignored and unimportant when I tell you that I am afraid of driving in the rain and you tell me there's nothing to worry about. I tell myself that you sound like my father used to when I was little and he didn't acknowledge me either.

FEELINGS AND COMFORT

I first recognized compulsive spending as a problem when I was counseling compulsive overeaters. Many of these people came from families where food was used as a panacea for hurts. The message was "eat this and it will make you feel good." I have seen parents at playgrounds who pick up a crying toddler who has just taken a spill and offer a sweet treat to stop the tears. If the child gets used to receiving treats as a way to make pain go away, he will think of food treats as a solution to all unhappiness. Even as an adult, this person may continue to use food to take away unhappy feelings.

When a child falls down and cries in pain and fear, and you distract the child with a treat or a toy, you are actually rejecting the child's feelings. You are unknowingly telling the toddler that there is nothing wrong when the child feels that there is really something wrong. The child may not be hurt but may feel scared or surprised. When you don't acknowledge his fear or hurt but distract his attention, you are teaching him to deny his feelings. Then, when he grows up, he will continue to soothe himself with a treat and continue to discount unhappy feelings that remain below the surface.

If the parent were to pick up the child, give him a hug and say, "I can see that you are upset. Let's look at your knee, wash it off, and see if you need a Band-Aid," the child would feel attended-to. The parent would be telling the toddler that what he feels is what he feels, and that it is okay to feel scared, but he can do something to make things fine without a treat or reward.

To recover from urges to spend or debt you will have to learn how to differentiate between emotional hunger and physical discomfort. The first step, when you are feeling carried away by your desire to spend, is to ask: "What's going on?" Keep asking this question and give yourself time to listen to your answers. You may still be upset or annoyed by an incident that happened twenty-four to forty-eight hours ago, even a week ago, and you have suppressed the anger, resentment, fear, or guilt. What has happened is that the emotional energy has built up to such an extent that it threatens to burst out. To comfort yourself, you find yourself thinking about "buying something."

What's going on? Some possible answers might be:

- My husband forgot my birthday.
- The mechanic said that fixing the car will cost $3500.
- My father is sick.
- I don't know how I'll pay my bills this month.
- I'm lonely without a love relationship in my life.

If you can recognize the feeling that goes with your unhappiness, such as angry, sad, demeaned, left out, surprised, frightened, helpless, overjoyed, you are making progress on your way to success.

UNDERSTANDING ANGER

When you feel threatened because someone or something is getting in the way of what you want, your body builds up energy. Your heartbeat speeds up; the system pumps out adrenalin. The body mobilizes for action against the enemy, but nothing happens because you think you can't or shouldn't act to confront the situation. Imagine what would happen if you assembled an army for battle, got them all combat-ready, and then called off the war, dismissing the troops without telling them where to go or what to do. The energy you have built up in your body to produce the "fight-or-flight" reaction is like that army. You are left feeling frustrated, resentful, or enraged. The anger energy needs an outlet or target. Some people swallow their anger and suffer psychosomatic illnesses, some turn their anger toward themselves, while others act out the anger on another person or object.

What were you taught about anger when you were growing up? Did you hear that anger was a bad thing and that you were a bad person if you felt angry? Many parents tell their children to "cut that out" when siblings are fighting or a child talks back. How do you turn off anger? If you try to stifle it, where does it go? Many compulsive spenders learned to push their angry feelings away and put on a happy face. Yet the anger was still there, just below the surface, like smoldering coals . . . not quite cold.

I learned at an early age to suppress my anger. In elementary school, I was known for my even temperament and was the person who helped others avoid fights and confrontations. As an adult, I believed that I never got angry. I didn't realize that my compulsive problems were temper tantrums. When I began to work to overcome my urges and cravings and went for psychotherapy, I finally uncovered my anger. What a surprise! I didn't know it was there.

Many compulsive bingers are oblivious to their anger. I remember the day I came face-to-face with being an angry person who had learned to hide it from herself and the world. It was a lovely Saturday, and my husband watched our small children so I could have some time to myself. I had a wonderful afternoon. When I came home, I went into the yard to greet my husband. He said, "What's wrong?" "Nothing is wrong," I replied. I remember thinking that it was odd for him to ask me that after the pleasant outing I had just had. He said, "You should see your face. You look very mad." I couldn't think of anything I was angry about, so I just shrugged it off. Three hours later I felt so angry about something that had happened that morning that I wanted to scream! My husband was right; I was angry, but I had become so adept at pushing it down that I had created a time delay.

As I worked to understand my inability to deal with anger appropriately, I discovered that I was terrified of anger. My fear was that I would discover a volcano of a lifetime of suppressed anger so great, that if it blew, if I let my anger out, it would destroy the entire planet. It took another year of therapy before I could be angry and feel angry simultaneously. When that happened I was both frightened and elated. I was frightened because I still thought showing anger was "bad" but happy that I didn't blow up civilization.

Anger is simply a feeling, just the same as happiness or sadness. When you suppress or deny resentment, anger or rage, you may develop other types of problems. You cannot live a life free of anger. You will encounter situations that make you mad. It is fine to accept that you are angry, but you are then responsible for your anger. When I ran a preschool we had a rule that we taught our toddlers: *People are not for hurting. Things are not for breaking.* It is not too late for you to practice these precepts.

Few of us ever were told how to handle anger. If you are so angry or resentful that you want to lash out but know you shouldn't, what can you do instead? Here are several ideas that have worked for others. Try hitting a large pillow and pretend it is the person you want to hit. Use your fists, feet, a baseball bat or tennis racket. Shout or scream until you are finished.

Some people feel better after they hit something like a kitchen counter with a rolled-up newspaper or a wrung-out wet towel. I have always enjoyed throwing ice cubes against my backyard wall because they shatter like glass but leave nothing to clean up.

Another suggestion to help you release the built up tension that accompanies angry feelings is screaming. Some people scream in the shower, while others find relief in screaming in their cars when the windows are rolled up. Once the white-hot feeling of rage has passed you will be in a better frame of mind to decide what to do next to resolve your problem.

"Dumping" is the act of venting your anger by hurling venomous words at another without thinking. This is an irresponsible behavior. I urge you to count to ten before you speak. Even better is to write an angry letter to the other person, but don't mail it. Use any language you choose in your letter. Reread your letter and think about the situation. You may decide to write a new letter using more civil communication or you may talk directly to the person in a calm and assertive manner, free of aggression.

Holding grudges rarely harms the other, but it will cause you emotional heartburn. In my book, *A Substance Called Food*, I told about a compulsive overeater named Edna. Although Edna was very overweight she had very shapely feet and was a compulsive shoe-buyer, with over eighty pair in her closet. She was also an anger collector. Edna loved to tell me about terrible things that people had done to her over thirty years ago. Each time she recalled these incidents she relived them and became angry and hurt all over again.

When I asked Edna how it helped her to keep these memories alive, feeling such intense anger, she replied, "It keeps me warm." Her anger and resentment acted like a shot of adrenalin in her body. The waves of rage made her feel alive.

Instead of asking Edna to write letters to the people in her stories, I gave her a pack of three-by-five cards and we listed the title of each angry memory with a brief description of the episode. She read them aloud one-by-one. After each card, I asked Edna if she was ready to let go of that experience. When she agreed, we burned the card.

After completing this ritual Edna began to behave differently. She learned to communicate her negative feelings promptly and has stopped using anger as an excuse to overeat or spend. Instead of dwelling on the worst in a situation or relationship, she is becoming more of an optimist.

THE ANGRY BOOK

Clean out the skeletons in your closet of bad feelings by writing an *Angry Book*. Get a notebook. The first step takes about fifteen minutes. Begin by listing all the people and events from your past and present that still make you feel angry or resentful. You will be surprised that you still feel angry toward the kids in your third grade class who picked you last for the team or your sister because she got more privileges than you. Name each event as if it were the title of a story in a table of contents. Don't describe the details. It will look like this:

- my fifth birthday party
- wearing Sara's hand-me-downs
- breaking up with Don
- I wasn't invited to Marian's dinner party
- my boss is showing favoritism toward George

Write down all your unfinished business, even if some people on your list are no longer alive. Your list doesn't have to be in chronological order.

Make an appointment to sit with yourself for fifteen minutes two or three times a week. When you start to write you may be angry at something that is not on your list. Begin with the current situation. When you are finished you can refer to your table of contents list. Start anywhere on your list. Pick a topic that appeals to you and begin to write. Spelling and grammar are not important because only you will see these pages. Put your book in a safe place to protect your personal thoughts. Use whatever language best expresses your feelings. While you are writing you may recall other topics or memories to add to your table of contents.

Each time you finish writing about a situation, read it over and write these two sentences at the bottom of the page:

I have discovered that . . .
I have decided to . . .

Keep writing until you have run out of topics and exhausted your grudge list. Then read the book and think about it. How do you feel? What do you want to do? You may want to write your decisions down as a list of activities to accomplish. Perhaps you will decide to share some of these revelations with a close friend, Twelve-Step sponsor, or therapist. When you have let go of all the garbage of the past, destroy the book. If any old angers return to haunt you, remind yourself that you have buried them, and they no longer can bother you.

Getting rid of old angers doesn't mean that you will be forever free of angry feelings. Events will occur in your life that you don't like. Keep current. Know your feelings, express them, and resolve them. Don't let angry sludge clog up your emotional system.

FACE YOUR FEAR

At the heart of anger is fear. After six years in an unhappy marriage, I found myself spending at my husband. I was enraged because he had trouble keeping a job, and we had constant money troubles. We had two small children, and, although I had a teaching credential, my parents had taught me to expect to marry a man who would support me in style so I wouldn't have to work after the children were born. My nagging and scolding simply played into my husband's feelings of inadequacy. If I pushed too far, it might lead to divorce. I was afraid that I couldn't support myself and two small children without his help, so I stayed and fumed and shopped. Shopping distracted me temporarily from my rage at my husband and my life.

Do you "spend at" someone you want to get even with or punish? When you spend, you dissipate the angry energy instead of honestly confronting the other person and addressing the real issues. Does angry spending help you or hurt you? What do you want to do to change?

When you consider talking to the other person face-to-face how do you feel, scared? Fear can keep you from expressing your feelings or telling the other what you really want. Perhaps you think that the other person will stop liking or loving you or will even punish you.

Most people I counsel believe that when they say no to someone they may hurt that person's feelings because they are disagreeing with another's wishes. You have a perfect right to you own wants and desires. Sometimes these do not comply with the other's plans, but that doesn't mean that you have to give in when you don't want to. When you tell yourself that you are responsible for making another person happy, you feel guilty because you believe the myth of: "If you loved me you would . . .. Since you won't do it, you don't love me." This isn't love! It is emotional blackmail.

Some common fears that affect compulsive spenders are: abandonment, change, looking foolish, rejection, pain, isolation, loss of love, financial problems, success, homelessness, sickness, failure, death. Give yourself time to think of each one. List them in the order of intensity with the scariest fear first and the least upsetting one last.

Write about each fear that you know is interfering with your life today. Is there some benefit you derive from living with this fear? Perhaps you get much attention from other people in your life. Does your fear control other people in some way? Can you imagine what would happen if you weren't consumed by your fear anymore? Reread what you have written and then complete this sentence: My new plan is . . ..

FEAR OF FAILURE

The two fears that seem to plague compulsive spenders are the fear of success and the fear of failure. Fear of failure is directly related to what others think of you or how they have the power to judge you. Fold a large piece of paper into four sections. Think of four people from your past and/or present life whose thoughts about you matter greatly. You may pick from among grandparents, aunts, uncles, parents, siblings, your children, neighbors, friends, or coworkers.

Put one name at the top of each section. Underneath each name list what that particular person wants from you or expects of you. Start each idea with the words, "I should." Cross out all the commands that others have given you that you don't agree with, things you don't want to do or choose to do. Shoulds are for children. It is how we teach them the rules of society. *Adults don't need to be driven by shoulds.*

Now look at the ideas you haven't crossed out. These are the things you feel good about expecting of yourself. Rewrite them on another paper using the words "I choose to" or "I want to" in front of each. An example would be: *I should* save money out of each paycheck becomes *I choose to* save money out of each paycheck.

There is a saying in Alcoholics Anonymous: "Don't judge your insides by other peoples' outsides." People with low self-esteem will invariably judge themselves as much worse than others. This enhances fear of failure. Cora, a compulsive shopper, confided in me that she felt better after a shopping spree because it gave her a sense of confidence she thought she was lacking. "When I buy things, I feel as if I can fit in," she said.

Do you judge your insides by other people's outsides? The next time you enter a room full of people, give yourself this task. Instead of dwelling on how different you are from everyone, look at all the ways you are similar to others. Begin with very simple things such as: we all have two eyes, sleep in beds, know how to write our names, watch TV, get wet when it rains, and want to be loved. Keep doing this wherever you go. Notice how your anxiety begins to disappear.

FEAR OF SUCCESS

Fear of success also can lead to self-destructive spending or debting. Some people believe that successful people become successful by harming others, taking what isn't theirs, cheating, or acting unlawfully.

Ted and Ben were afraid of being too rich. Ted believed that money corrupts, and rich people are mean and heartless. If he allowed himself to keep the money he earned he would be in danger of becoming wealthy and would turn into a despicable man. Ben told me that rich people benefit because they deprive others who remain poor. Rich people are unethical and ruthless. Why would anyone want to be like that? Both these men let money run through their fingers. Therefore they never had enough to become rich.

One client worried that once she had "made it" there would be nothing left in life. While she was in debt and had to struggle, she would never have to find out if her fantasy was the truth. If you secretly feel unworthy or bad, you may be unable to allow yourself to have money or keep money. Compulsive spending or debting will surely keep you from your goal.

What are your thoughts and beliefs about rich or successful people? Take a few minutes now and think about people you have known or heard about who are rich or successful. Do you want to be like them? What words come to mind: glamour, ease, comfort, having everything, playing, cheating, mean, in danger, workaholic, brilliant? Is that who you must be? How does that make you feel?

Do you have permission to be successful or wealthy? Who would feel disappointed or abandoned if you succeeded? Do you secretly consider yourself a fraud? Are you afraid that others would find out something awful about you if you were successful?

Fear of independence can influence your behavior. Spending to stay poor is often a sign of low self-worth. Although Toni was a talented and intelligent artist, she only found jobs that paid minimum wage. She secretly feared that if her talent as an artist was discovered, she might have to live up to other people's expectations. What if she wasn't good enough? Staying poor kept her from finding out.

FEAR OF LOSS OF LOVE

A message my generation received was that women should be taken care of by men. Therefore, it was okay for women to be frivolous with money, be air heads about finance, and never earn more than a man. Some women still are unconsciously influenced by these outmoded beliefs and remain helpless, asking to be rescued, because they are afraid of losing their feminine identity. For these women love and financial support are synonymous. They are worried that if they take care of themselves economically, they will appear not to need love or money.

Fear of the loss of love is a common feeling that motivates both men and women to go into debt. Countless compulsive spenders equate buying things with "love." Love is often expressed through gifts and cash. I have already mentioned Gary, whose parents seemed to reward him when he was down-and-out, but became cold and judgmental when he was financially solvent.

Compulsive spending and debting is a way to avoid intimacy too. Never having enough or earning enough is an excuse for not being in a committed relationship. "When I get out of debt I'll get married" seems like a valid statement, but may hide a fear of getting close. Compulsive spending keeps people from saving for a secure future. Then they feel inadequate because they never seem to have enough, which makes them insecure, and they spend to assuage feelings of unhappiness. It is a vicious circle.

NEGATIVE FEELINGS

Many people are not aware that they are depressed, yet suffer from a sense of hopelessness and lack of joy in their lives. If you are seriously depressed and find that you are not sleeping well and are having trouble functioning in your daily life—sometimes feeling too low even to get out of the house—see your doctor for diagnosis and treatment.

Depression and anger are often interrelated. Under the depressed feelings you may find unexpressed anger.

Sometimes the anger is so strong that you shut down all feelings to contain the rage, so that you are aware only of your lethargy. You may see your life as impossible and unchangeable. Feelings of hopelessness and helplessness result. Shopping and spending are ways that some people fight depression, but they provide only short-lived distractions.

Boredom is a second cousin to depression. A common excuse for binge buying is boredom, "I had nothing to do, so I went shopping." Boredom is not a primary feeling, but it is a way of covering over other feelings. Refer to the list of feelings provided earlier in this chapter and find the ones that may be beneath the surface of your boredom. You could be suppressing anxiety, resentment, fear, guilt, or sadness.

Strong feelings of guilt contribute to many binges. If compulsive spenders aren't feeling guilty before the compulsive act, they usually feel guilty afterward or when they get the bill. Guilt is a waste of time! Guilt comes from not living up to someone else's expectations, your *shoulds* or *shouldn'ts*. One of my favorite sayings is: "What other people think about me is none of my business." If you are willing to be responsible for the outcome of your decisions and your behavior, you no longer need to feel guilty. I do not say this to endorse compulsive spending or debting, but to point out that when you begin to live life on your terms, eliminating guilt, you will begin to make new decisions.

SELF-DISCOUNT LEADS TO SELF-DEBTING

If you have completed the assignments I have suggested so far, you now are better acquainted with the four basic feelings: mad, glad, sad, and scared. Many compulsive people cannot describe what they feel, but they minimize the intensity of the feeling; they lie to themselves about how upset they are. I call that "self-discount." Discount stores are wonderful because we can buy fine items marked down in price. A self-discount is the process of marking yourself down. When you don't let yourself be as good as others, get what others seem to attract with ease, or even let yourself know that it is okay to feel the feelings others feel, you are devaluing yourself.

When you lie to yourself about how much something hurts you, angers you, or worries you, it is like walking away from a fire without extinguishing it. The burning embers may reignite and flame. Feelings that are not acknowledged and resolved flair up as a spending binge.

Whenever I hear a client describe her behavior as childish or silly, I know she is discounting herself. How are grownups supposed to act anyway, and when are we mandated to cut off letting the child spirit within each of us enjoy life? I usually ask, "Whose voice do you hear telling you that's silly?" In our childhood our caregivers were often people who knew nothing about child development or psychology.

A Self-Help Program for Change

A twenty-one-year-old student with a spending problem told me that she is the selfish one in the family. "Why is that?" I asked. She assured me that it is true because when she was very tiny she wouldn't share her toys. Her mother labeled her "selfish," and the family accepted that judgment. I assured the young woman that all very young children don't share. It is normal and natural. As the child grows, she learns to share some toys, and it is also fine to keep others in a special private place. I remember that my daughter at the age of two had a toy guitar she cherished. When another child came to visit we would store it away while her playmate was present. They played happily with the other toys.

You are not silly or childish when you feel jealous, angry or frightened, though you wish you didn't feel that way. Feelings do not need to be justified. You feel your feelings because of what you are telling yourself about things and people. After you accept that you are indeed jealous, it doesn't make you a bad person, just human. You can learn to transform unwanted feelings by dialoguing with your inner critic and learning how to rewrite your inner self-talk.

When you compare yourself to others and find yourself "less than," you may hide your feelings from them for fear of their judgment. Perhaps an adult taught you that it isn't polite to let others know your inner feelings, especially those that might be embarrassing because they show that you are imperfect.

Every time you hear yourself say "It doesn't matter" when someone asks you for your preference, you are putting yourself down. You are telling others that they are more important and more worthy than you, and your opinions don't count. Later you may suffer from a headache, upset stomach or go on a spending binge because you didn't express your true feelings and wants because of your fear of rejection or disapproval.

If you think that the situation is hopeless and there's nothing you can do to change things, you also may stifle your feelings. Maureen had her hands full with five children. She asked her husband to participate more, but although he agreed, he seldom followed through. Finally Maureen decided that the family needed therapy. Her husband absolutely refused to go or to pay for counseling. Maureen felt powerless because she didn't work. She was totally dependent on her husband. He wielded all the power.

Maureen's way of dealing with her feelings was to shop. Spending enabled her to reward herself for having to put up with things, and it was a sly way of getting even with her husband by costing him money after all.

People who deny or suppress their negative feelings because they feel unworthy are often self-debtors. They treat themselves badly, using their money for others and denying themselves fine things. They rarely buy themselves new things, and usually the item has to be on sale or a special bargain. Self-debtors act second best.

Learning to admit your negative feelings to yourself and to share them with others will cause rapid change in overcoming your self-defeating compulsive behavior. Listen to your talk. Be alert for the times you say something is silly, childish or doesn't matter. The sentence, "It doesn't bother me," really means it does bother me, but I feel inadequate because it shouldn't bother me. If you pretend that things are fine when they aren't, you will continue to spend compulsively.

Anger, guilt, fear, and resentment seem like great tidal waves that overwhelm you. You spend or debt as a way of suppressing or lessening emotional pain. The key to the problem lies elsewhere, in finding the source of your feelings. When you learn to change how you *think* you will change what you feel and control how you act.

8

LISTEN TO YOUR THOUGHTS

When I was first dating my husband we had a terrible disagreement. I felt hurt and discounted by him, and I told him about it. He explained his side of things, but I still wasn't satisfied. I was very, very angry. I insisted on holding onto my hurt. Finally, he said something that took me completely by surprise. He asked me when I would be finished with my anger.

My first reaction was, "How should I know?" I told him that I had no idea how long I would rage, but he persisted and explained to me that I was creating the anger, and therefore I could choose to curtail it anytime I wished. He insisted that I set a deadline. Finally, I grudgingly owned that I couldn't think of being happy for at least 36 hours. "Fine," he said, "I'll be back tomorrow when you're finished!" Sure enough, I was fine by the next evening.

That was a very important experience in my life. I no longer allow the people I counsel to believe that they are powerless over their feelings, not just anger but sadness, guilt, fear, or anxiety. Feelings are not like the clouds in the sky that seem to just appear, move along, and disappear. We turn them on. We also can turn them off.

What starts a feeling, and what stops it? Your thoughts and your beliefs give birth to your feelings. You create your happiness and your misery because of your view of the world and yourself. If you live in an area where floods are a danger, you will feel anxious when the rains come because you are telling yourself that you may suffer from the disaster of losing your home. But if you live in a drought-ridden part of the country, you will rejoice at the first sign of rain because you are telling yourself that help is at hand to relieve the water shortage.

Repeated spending and debting results from dysfunctional attitudes and perceptions about money and self. We each have a little voice inside our head that talks to us day and night. We are so used to it that we rarely let others in on our private dialogue. You may have heard it called your "self-talk." What you tell yourself in the privacy of your head drastically influences how you feel and what you do. You will change your behavior with spending and debting when you change the ideas and the commands you give yourself.

LISTEN TO YOUR SELF-TALK

You have lived with your inner voice all your life so you have never questioned whether it speaks the truth. Much of what you think of as the truth is only your opinion. A belief is merely a self-affirming theory. We tell ourselves that it is true because many of us agree that it is, not because we have proof. To learn how to differentiate between truth and harmful opinions you will have to check your self-talk out with a trusted friend or counselor. In this chapter I will teach you how to reevaluate your thoughts and how to rewrite them into positive and life-affirming ideas.

Start right now by remembering the last time you had a shopping spree or had to fight off the desire to spend. Can you recall what situation or relationship was upsetting you? How did you feel about it?

I felt . . .(*mad, glad, sad, scared*). . . because I was telling myself . . ..

Gail's husband spent more money on his Christmas present for their poodle than he spent on her gift. She was furious and spent at him to get even. When Gail got the bills she was filled with remorse because of her spending binges. Gail would respond to the sample sentences this way:

"I felt angry at Christmas when you spent more money on the dog than you did on me because I was telling myself that you don't love me and you were punishing me."

A Self-Help Program for Change

As time went on Gail became more conscious that her spending tantrums coincided with times her husband discounted or ignored her. He often worked late or found excuses to be away. She felt lonely and unappreciated. She soothed herself with trips to the mall. As Gail started to ask for what she wanted, she could control her urges to shop. Eventually she convinced her husband to go for marital counseling to work out their problems.

Sherry had a different set of beliefs. Sherry earned a wonderful salary, and loved expensive things. She lived in a high rent apartment and rarely said no to her whims. Her goal was to save enough money for a down payment on a home, but she was far from her goal. Sherry had been brought up in a conventional family where the man was the financial manager and the woman was the recipient of his largesse. Dad seemed to know all about money while Mom was somewhat of an air head when the word investment was mentioned.

As Sherry became more and more frustrated at the way she sabotaged her intention to save, she finally began to explore her thoughts and beliefs. When she completed the sentences she discovered this: "I feel happy when I spend money on the things I like because I'm telling myself that I don't have to worry about saving. Some strong, smart man will come along and take care of everything like my dad did."

Sherry discovered that there were two negative beliefs at work in her life: "Money brings hassles" and

"You don't have to know about those things." Once Sherry understood that those were really her mother's reactions, she could let go of them and make learning about money and investing money effectively her business.

THE GARDEN OF LIFE PHILOSOPHY

I think the world is like a garden; we are all like its flowers and plants. Some people are roses or violets; others are like shrubs or wildflowers. Some are weeds or vegetables. Gail, who spent at her husband, was expecting him to be a rose. In fact, he was an onion. She kept feeling disappointed and angry when he didn't act like a rose. A rose would want to spend much time with her and buy her surprises, spend large amounts of money on her. Onions aren't romantic. Onions may act prosaic most of the time and be somewhat dull.

During marital counseling Gail learned to stop expecting her spouse to be a rose and began to look at some positive qualities of an onion. Instead of expecting him to buy her sexy underwear as a present, she realized that onions often buy toasters and blenders as birthday presents. It's their way of showing they care. Gail learned that if she wanted sexy undies, she would have to communicate her wishes to him and stop expecting him to read her mind.

When you view the world as a great garden and all the people in your life as a wonderful variety of plants, you can stop being upset or frustrated if they don't change when you want them to change. Gail often soothed her hurt feelings with a shopping spree after a bout with her mother-in-law. No matter what she did or said, her mother-in-law criticized or embarrassed her. Clearly her mother-in-law was a cactus! I asked Gail to make up a checklist of her mother-in-law's most irritating cactus habits or words that Gail reacted to repeatedly. Instead of cringing and waiting for the ax to fall and for feelings of inadequacy to fill her, I taught Gail to wait expectantly for the prickly barbs about her parenting skills, how badly she dressed her children, what poorly behaved children they were, and what a bad housekeeper she was.

We made a game of this. As Gail kept track of her mother-in-law's complaints, she laughed instead of crying over the criticisms. She could see how very cactus-like her mother-in-law really was. Whenever the older woman said something especially insulting, Gail learned to take a deep breath and quietly remind herself, "That is just your *opinion*. It is not the *truth* about me. Cactuses are like that." Once Gail took back the power she had given her mother-in-law she could spend time with her and feel comfortable. She no longer had to comfort herself with spending binges as a reward for putting up with the old witch.

You cannot change other people, but you can learn to stop expecting them to change, and you can learn to stop feeling helpless about it. You have three choices: 1) continue to feel powerless and binge over it, 2) learn how to change your ideas and thoughts so you can let people be themselves without feeling resentful, and 3) change the situation by removing yourself from it.

Remind yourself that *your thoughts precede your feelings*. You control your feelings to the extent that you can listen in on your thoughts and opinions and evaluate them. If you have spent your life being carried away by your feelings, you may say things you later regret. Or you may be someone who stifles what you wish to say or do.

You can practice using your power to decide how you feel, what you think, and how you want to resolve the problem. Gail allowed herself to feel hurt by her mother-in-law's comments because she assumed that her mother-in-law had the power to judge her as "lovable" and give her the stamp of approval. When Gail realized that her mother-in-law's ideas were only opinions and not the truth, she could take back her power and no longer felt inadequate. Her mother-in-law's criticism began to roll of her back, like rain off a duck.

If you think that others should be as considerate, sensitive, loyal, and reasonable as you are, you are expecting the world to be your clone. It may not seem fair, but each of us is unique. Some are more loving, some more capable, some more honest than others.

When I was first married, my husband often pointed out that I was very difficult to buy gifts for because I usually beat him to it and bought what I wanted for myself. Somewhere my small inner child had the negative expectation that no one would get me exactly what I wanted and I would be inconsolable. To prevent this fantasy of misery from happening, I got myself what the child within wanted. Although I felt secure, I was also acting out of mistrust, a behavior that jeopardized my relationship, since I wasn't giving my husband a chance to act loving.

WHAT ARE YOUR RIGHTS?

Compulsive spenders and debtors suffer from low self-esteem. If you believe that you are not adequate, good, lovable, or capable, you will not allow yourself to feel happy. Unhappiness, lack of self-confidence, and depression lead to compulsive abuse of money and credit. When you change your beliefs, you can alter your mood and your actions will be productive and positive.

If you have a history of letting others have their way without putting up a fight, saying yes when you are thinking no, you are a nonassertive person. Binges seem to give you the good feelings you let yourself miss out on because you give away your rights and don't stand up for your wants and beliefs but rather do whatever is necessary to avoid making waves.

On the following pages are eight specific personal rights that you may be telling yourself don't apply to you. As you read them, you may feel extremely uncomfortable about certain ones. Your recovery depends on learning to accept that these rights are yours too. First read through all the rights. Make a mark next to the ones that make you uneasy. Take each you marked and write your thoughts and your excuses for disallowing it. You will discover how your opinions about yourself are holding you back and creating frustration and a feeling of powerlessness.

• I HAVE THE RIGHT TO PUT MYSELF FIRST.

Do you think that putting yourself first is selfish? If you do, you may have let other people pick up on your belief in your inadequacy and take advantage of you. When you think you are responsible for other people's happiness before yours, you are doomed to be treated like a servant and to feel invisible around those people. When will it be your turn to stop being taken for granted and have happiness or fun?

Lisa was an adult child of an alcoholic father who constantly abused the family, both physically and verbally. She grew up with very low self-esteem. The way Lisa described her behavior with money was, "It burns a hole in my pocket." During counseling, using hypnosis and guided imagery, we explored and healed the traumas of her early childhood. Lisa discovered that she learned to think of herself as unworthy. Coming from a shame-based life view, she came to understand that she had to get rid of her money because "I don't deserve it." As Lisa learned to honor herself and put herself first, she rewrote her belief and affirmed, "I deserve the very best."

- I HAVE THE RIGHT TO BE THE JUDGE OF MY FEELINGS AND TO ACCEPT THEM AS HUMAN.

When you doubt that you have permission to feel what you feel and that your feelings are legitimate, you are engaging in self-discount. Believing that others know you better than you know yourself, leads you to constantly suppress feelings or judge yourself as "bad." Judging your feelings as bad or silly keeps you stuck in a depressed frame of mind.

- I HAVE THE RIGHT TO MAKE MISTAKES.

- I HAVE THE RIGHT TO CHANGE MY MIND OR CHOOSE A DIFFERENT COURSE OF ACTION.

I have put these two together because a person who doesn't allow himself to make mistakes cannot change his mind either. This is the problem of perfectionists who tell themselves that there is only one right way . . . and they don't know what it is. Anything they do may be wrong. This is like the old saying, "You made your bed, and now you must lie in it!" This means that once they choose a path they cannot stop, even if it proves uncomfortable or incorrect.

For years I have been looking for a perfect person. I have yet to find anyone who never errs. If nobody is perfect, why do you have to be? We seem to learn best from our mistakes. As a therapist who works with compulsive behaviors I encourage my clients to observe that the most awful spree may be one of the best teachers you can have. Understand what creates your cravings and urges to spend money and your recovery will be swift.

Here and now I want to give you permission to ignore the advice of others. As a People-pleaser you have pushed aside your innermost dreams because you are usually thinking that someone else knows more, is luckier, or more deserving. It is now time for you to risk doing things your way. If you disagree with the opinion or advice of someone important in your life, ask yourself what is the worst thing that could happen if you followed your preferred path. What do you think the outcome would be? If you are willing to find out, go ahead and do what you really want.

- I HAVE THE RIGHT TO BE ALONE, EVEN WHEN OTHERS WANT MY COMPANY.

- I HAVE THE RIGHT TO SAY "NO."

People-pleasers often feel resentment toward those they go along with. No other human being can read your mind to know what you really want. If you need time for yourself, not even your spouse or your closest friend will know unless you speak up.

People-pleasers often find themselves in situations that are especially risky. Kit was out with friends who wanted to go to a swap meet. She knew that she would lose control but was ashamed to say that she didn't want to go for fear that the others would probe and she would have to reveal her compulsive problem. She went along and bought merchandise she didn't want with money she couldn't afford. The result was depression and self-hatred.

Kit learned that it is better in the long run to say no. In the future she will be more assertive. If she is outvoted she will stay home rather than put herself in jeopardy.

- I HAVE THE RIGHT TO NOT TAKE RESPONSIBILITY FOR SOMEONE ELSE'S PROBLEM OR HAPPINESS.

In recent years we have been hearing the word "codependency" frequently. Codependents take on other people's problems and try to fix them. They spend so much time and energy worrying, fixing, and feeling, that they are often depressed and tired. One way to cheer themselves up is to buy things. Shopping binges are unconscious ways to reward yourself for the drudgery of your life or relationship.

Olivia tearfully reported that she had given away an inheritance because she couldn't turn down hard-luck stories. She felt obligated to help needy people. Thus, others often took advantage of her. She didn't give thought to her needs and her future security, and found herself out-of-money and feeling victimized.

- I HAVE THE RIGHT TO ASK OTHERS FOR HELP OR SUPPORT.

Compulsive spenders tell me that they are smart enough to know better and should be able to overcome the problem alone through willpower. This is self-discount again. These same people realize that they don't have the skill or knowledge necessary to remove their appendix or fix their plumbing. Most of us have permission to ask for help when the problem is mechanical repair or ill health, but we are ashamed to admit psychological difficulties. Recovery hinges on getting yourself to admit that you have been unable to do it yourself and it is okay to reach out for support.

Review the eight Personal Rights I have discussed. Take a few moments to think about which ones you want to allow yourself to accept more easily. Complete each of these phrases with ten different endings.

I have the right to be _____
I have the right to do _____
I have the right to have _____
I have the right to stop _____

When you take action from a position of power and choice you will leave guilt and shame behind.

YOUR SELF-IMAGE

Compulsive people are usually all-or-nothing people. They tell themselves that they have only two choices:

"either" and "or." Paul was a master of self-debting. He was a charming man who spent his energy looking for work but never seemed to find it. Meanwhile, through his winning ways, he found many love-hungry women who were glad to give him a place to live while he "got it together." Paul was living with his latest girlfriend, to whom he was very attached, but he was getting tired of being a pauper.

He had many creative ideas, was young and strong, but couldn't seem to find the "proper work." Eventually we discovered that his self-sabotaging behavior stemmed from a hidden belief that he could have *either* love *or* money, but not both! Each time he fell in love he preferred the warmth and caring of the relationship and secretly feared that he would lose that love if he were successful. His self-debting reflected his belief that he deserved less in life than most other people.

By limiting yourself to only two choices, both of which are inadequate to solve your dilemma, you will feel stuck and continue to overspend as a way of relieving your frustration and powerlessness. Some of the polarities you offer yourself are: good or bad, perfect or failure, attractive or ugly, and loved or unloved.

You have been practicing all-or-nothing thinking all your life. Make a game of listening to yourself. When you catch yourself in a black-or-white, all-or-nothing phrase, avoid putting yourself down with harsh judgment and, instead, give yourself credit for noticing the error.

This irrational and destructive way of thinking is rampant in our society. Because we don't know that there is another way, we are plagued by unhappy feelings that arise from limited choices. These feelings create the desire to spend. We received both verbal and nonverbal messages from our caregivers as we were growing up. As children, these messages seemed like "commands" to us. Things that were repeated over and over told you that you were a "difficult" child or that you were a "perfect angel," "Daddy's little helper," or "scatterbrained." You may still be acting in ways that justify that label though you are an adult. That is called a "self-fulfilling prophesy." Your self-image as a lovable or unlovable person may even stem from the stories you were told about your birth.

Here is an activity that will enable you to understand how you developed the image of who you think you are. Take as much time as you need to think about each question and write your answers. You may want to contact relatives to obtain some information you don't recall.

MY PERSONAL HISTORY

1. What were you told about your birth? Were you wanted? Were you an accident? Were you the preferred sex? Were your parents happy about your birth? What decision did you make about yourself after knowing this?

2. What were you told about the delivery? Did Mother have a hard time or an easy time? Were you early, late or on time? You may have earned the reputation as "the pushy one who couldn't wait to be here" or "the lazy one who took his time arriving." Were there complications during or after birth for you or Mother? Who was there? What have you decided about yourself from learning this information?

3. What was happening in your family and their world at the time of your birth? Were your parents happy? Were there other children? Were your parents having money or health problems at the time? What was going on in the world: peace, war, plenty, scarcity? How did these conditions affect you?

4. What were you told about your infancy? Were you a "good" baby or troublesome? Did you have colic, allergies, illnesses? Did you cry too much, eat too little? Who took care of you? How did your siblings react to you? What decision did you make about yourself?

5. What kind of personality or special traits did you exhibit? Were you given nicknames? Were you labeled as bright, beautiful, musical, happy, rebellious, curious, too-smart-for-your-own-good, friendly, or sickly? Compare your labels with those given your brothers or sisters. You will discover that all of you may be continuing to live up to them still. If you are the baby of the

family you may be treated as such even if you are over forty.

6. Look at photographs of yourself as a child. What memories do you recall as you look at them? Compare what you see with what you were told. Often individuals who call themselves ugly from childhood find out they were adorable but were labeled less than acceptable because they were compared with another child or because they had a personality or energy level that was deemed unacceptable by that family. What have you just discovered?

Some messages you received were positive and some were negative or vague. "You are just like your father" might have meant that you were a good athlete, a born leader, a moody person, a spendthrift, or many other things. Think about the relatives you were compared to? What were their qualities or traits? Is this the truth about you? In what ways are you like some of these people? In what ways are you different?

Gilbert was a smart businessman whose business was starting to be in trouble because of his self-defeating behavior. He procrastinated about following up on orders and keeping records correctly. The upshot was that the IRS was breathing down his neck, and he was in a state of panic. Gilbert was often told he was like his father and grandfather. As Gilbert thought about it, the phrase that came to mind was that Grandpa had lived life "behind the eight ball." Gilbert's dad also lived life "behind the eight ball." Both men liked to create situations that were risky, but they managed to sail through and succeed. Gilbert realized that he too had created a situation where he was "behind the eight ball," but he was not succeeding.

Whether you realize it or not, the decisions you have made because of your experiences, the verbal and nonverbal commands handed down by your parents, teachers and other caretakers, and the influences of society helped you create a unique and personal life script for yourself. Your view of the world and the part you have written for yourself in your personal soap opera need to be reevaluated now in order for you to decide to do things differently.

One technique you can use to uncover this life script is to list as many "shoulds" as you can. Shoulds are handed down to us as a way of teaching us what is acceptable in our family and community. As adults we often discover that "should" means "I don't want to, but they are making me." Here are suggested topics to write about. Under each write down all the "shoulds" or "want-me-tos" that you can think of.

SHOULDS about: men, women, children, mothers, fathers, sisters, brothers, lovers, friends, being *good*.

SHOULDS I have received from others. Tell what each want you to do or be: mother, father, sister, brothers, spouse, my children, my best friend, my boss, my church, the government, my neighbors.

SHOULDS about life. What do I demand of myself about these topics: spending money, saving money, using money, earning money, spending time, wasting time, sex, success, good manners, honesty, friendship, love?

When you have completed this set of questions, carefully read your answers and ponder them. What have you discovered? What changes are you willing to make to alleviate depression, guilt, shame, or anger?

In this time of awareness of the prevalence of child abuse and incest, a common sources of conflict is the belief: "Of course I should love them because they are my parents." When a child has been beaten, insulted, sexually abused or abandoned by a parent and tries to talk herself into loving that person, she is left with enormous guilt for being unable to feel love. Trying to force yourself through guilt to love what has been destructive is crazy making.

I have developed a rule about relatives. I suggest that you ask yourself, if those people were your neighbors down the street, what kind of relationship would you want to have with them? Parents have to earn love from their children. You do not have to love an unlovable person. Trying to force yourself to love a person who has mistreated you can lead to physical illness or emotional pain. Sometimes getting a divorce from one or both of your parents is the only way to achieve peace of mind.

SELF-TALK CREATES FEELINGS

Fear, rejection, low self-worth, loneliness, and anger are the most common triggers of spending binges. You can learn to defuse these feelings when you learn to examine the underlying thoughts that generated them and change those thoughts.

Rejection occurs when you tell yourself that someone doesn't like you or want a relationship with you. If a friend turns down a simple request to join you at the movies because of another obligation, do you take it as a rejection? If a friend or fellow worker disagrees with you, is that rejection? You may convince yourself that your parents or spouse don't love you because they don't want to accept your irresponsible behavior and demand that you change.

Believing that you are being rejected because something is wrong with you, erodes your self-esteem as you convince yourself that you are not a likable or capable person. If you had a childhood in which you were deprived of love, approval, or material comfort, you may mistakenly be expecting people in your adult life to make up for all you missed. When they don't or can't, you may feel angry or depressed and go out and spend on yourself.

Many compulsive eaters and purgers talk about the feeling of the "bottomless pit," a void that aches to be filled yet never feels satisfied, no matter how much they eat. The void is one that cannot be filled with things because it represents an emptiness from long ago that gets reproduced in the present. Compulsive spenders share this experience.

Caroline and her husband were looking for a larger house because she had collected so many works of art and antiques there wasn't any more room in their present house. Caroline had an insatiable need to have things. She was an illegitimate child who had been emotionally neglected in childhood. Somehow she felt as if even God had disowned her. Buying and surrounding herself with pretty things was her only way to console herself, but it was temporary because her real need to feel loved and appreciated belonged to the small child within. She tried to ignore or deny that child's needs just as she was ignored a long time ago.

Loneliness is a prevalent problem in today's society. People with a shaky self-image doubt that others genuinely want to be with them. They can feel lonely in the midst of a crowd because their self-talk is about how stupid, ugly, shy or bad they really are. Some women believe that they can't be happy unless they have a mate.

I recall a conversation with Norma Jean, a college student whose buying binges reflected her state of mind. It was April, and college would be over for the year at the end of May. Norma Jean was disconsolate because she had broken up with her last boyfriend and hadn't replaced him. "If I don't have a boyfriend by the end of May, I won't have any fun until next September," she said. When I asked her to explain her thoughts she said, "The only place to meet men is on the campus. If I don't meet someone before school is out I'll be stuck."

Norma Jean and I spent the hour exploring her all-or-nothing thinking. She finally realized that there might be some eligible men outside school, and that men wanted to meet women every month of the year. Although she didn't have a new man in her life when school was over, I am happy to report that Norma Jean had a very social summer.

Anger, frustration, fear and depression are the result of magical thinking. Magical thinking means that you act as if you had the miraculous ability to predict the future. The rub is that the future you are predicting is always filled with tragedy and negative outcomes.

Betsy was a compulsive debtor who had finally declared bankruptcy. Then she began to live within her means and curb her urges to shop. She had been doing very well when one rainy day, on the way to work, she was hit by an uninsured motorist. Betsy was a professional typist. In the accident her hand was broken. She called me after she had returned from the doctor and hysterically poured out her story. The doctor told her she would have to go on disability. Betsy sobbed as she declared that she would lose her job, be unable to pay her rent or car payment, and end up homeless. She was sure these dire happenings would come to pass. In fact, none of this happened. Her bosses asked her to be the receptionist while her hand healed. Her salary continued, and she could remain solvent.

Along with magical thinking goes another magician's trick called mind reading, which most of us indulge in. Mind reading means that we think we know what another person is thinking or feeling, and we are so sure of our negative conclusions that we don't bother to check it out.

Barbie was a typical mind reader. She used to spend at her husband because he didn't get her presents for special occasions. Instead he would give her money. Barbie decided that he didn't want to take the time to think of something personal that would please her because he no longer loved her. She dreaded each Mother's Day, anniversary, or birthday. I asked Barbie to bring her husband Len to a session so we could check out her beliefs.

Len explained that the worst thing he could think of was to receive a gift that he didn't like and couldn't return. To save people from that kind of unhappiness, Len decided to give money so the person could get exactly what would please her. He considered his action a sign of great caring and sensitivity. Barbie was amazed when she found this out. The result was that they decided to go shopping together. Barbie could begin to show Len the kinds of things she liked, and she would feel that he was really interested. She expressed her wish that soon he could risk buying her something as a surprise.

As you practice listening in to your self-talk you will find it easier and easier to see the connection between the thought and the feeling that results. The more familiar you become with the process of rewriting your thoughts, the happier you will feel and the more power you will have over your life.

BE A POSITIVE THINKER

Throughout this chapter I have been pointing out the way that your thoughts and beliefs trigger intense feelings of anger, fear, or depression. These in turn lead to the acts of compulsive spending and debting. To succeed, you must become an expert eavesdropper and listen in on your inner voice. You may be amazed and unhappily surprised to find that you think of the world in negative terms.

A very easy way to turn negative thinking around is through self-affirmations. An affirmation is simply a positive statement. TV commercials are filled with affirmation, as are prayers and proverbs. You can use some of these or make up new ones. Beware of negative affirmations. These are statements in which you reinforce a negative belief as if it were positive. An example is someone who tells you that they are "unlucky in love," or "always losing things."

Self-affirmations command your unconscious just like a computer program. You can change the software program in your computer by changing the disk. I prefer to think of my unconscious as the genie of the magic lamp in the story of Aladdin. The genie told Aladdin, "I am the slave of the lamp. Your wish is my command."

You see, genies must obey, no matter what. The unconscious is like that genie. It fulfills your command, positive or negative. You are like Aladdin. What you think about yourself is a wish that will then come true.

You are already using positive affirmations. If you need a new television set or washing machine you will find yourself thinking about it and imagining how you will enjoy it when you buy it. You will be looking in the newspaper for ads and even shopping to find out the different options and prices. While you are considering this venture, you don't doubt that the new item will be yours because there are thousands of appliances available.

Most of us take it for granted that we will have material goods like clothing, furniture, and cars, yet most of the people I see forget to use this positive technique to acquire health, loving relationships, and happiness.

You may want to start by choosing a favorite adage or prayer that makes you feel good. Original affirmations work as well, but make them short and to the point. What works best for me is to say affirmations out loud quietly, but firmly, to myself. I only use one or two at a time, and say each at least ten times.

I have made a habit of self-affirmations by doing it at the same time every day, usually when I am doing something like taking a shower or driving my car. Some people report success when they write out each affirmation ten times. One man liked to carry a small index card with a few affirmations that he said as he jogged every day.

Here are some affirmations others have enjoyed using:

- I deserve the very best.
- I am a lovable and capable person.
- I choose to be the master of my fate.
- I now welcome loving relationships into my life.

Saying affirmations out loud or writing them is easy to do and will soon become a daily habit. But not all your affirmations will succeed. Take another look at the affirmations that seem stalled. You may have an unconscious fear of allowing yourself to have what you think you want.

Here is a simple way to find out if you are stopping yourself. Take a piece of paper and write your affirmation on the top. Say it aloud: "It's okay for me to make mistakes." Now say "Yes but ..." What is the doubting critical voice within telling you in rebuttal? It could be, "You make too many mistakes already" or "People will find out you are stupid." Write that down. Now say the positive affirmation a second time and listen for the next "yes but" that you hear in your mind, for example "We don't make mistakes in this family." Again, write it down. Keep announcing the affirmation and write the rebuttals until you truly have run out of "yes buts." Then write the affirmation ten times.

During one of my workshops Virginia created an affirmation that said, "It is okay for me to have money come to me that I don't earn." When she tried to use it, she felt very uncomfortable. After using the "yes but" technique, she revealed to herself that the critical inner voice was telling her "You don't deserve it. You are not worth it."

I have already mentioned Maureen, who got back at her husband by spending. Maureen was from Ireland and grew up in a poor family of twenty children. She came to the United States and got married. Her home was stuffed with furniture and bric-a-brac. Her children always looked neat. But everything she bought was secondhand or from a thrift store. She bought compulsively and spent large sums of money. After Maureen did this exercise she came up with the belief "I don't deserve *new* things." This made sense in light of her childhood, but she was now in a different country and married to a man who supported her well.

It is time you stopped living in the problem and begin to live in the answer. The problem is your irrational thinking and negative belief system. If you are depressed, anxious, or have the urge to spend, chances are you are thinking yourself into a binge. Whenever possible, write down your twisted thoughts and practice challenging them. See if you can come up with valid and positive alternatives. Listen for the negative voice that will try to sabotage you. Fight back until you have let go of the old ways of thinking. As you change your thoughts, you will change your life.

9

MAKING IT WORK

The STOP, LOOK, LISTEN program for change can work when *you* work it. I know that you know what to do and how to do it, but you don't know that you know. Spending sprees and throwing money around can often be traced to a feeling of powerlessness over a situation or relationship. When you are frustrated because things don't go your way, your needs aren't being met, and others don't want to "shape up," it seems as if things will never change. These thoughts create the unhappiness that can lead to buying yourself something to cheer yourself up. I call this state of mind "Ain't it awful, and there's nothing I can do about it!"

Many compulsive people who feel like victims of fate eagerly look around for someone to fix them. There is no magic pill to eliminate cravings. No policeman can keep you *good*. You must now heal yourself. Spending and debting are your ineffective ways of coping with uncomfortable feelings and situations.

INNER WISDOM

There is wisdom within you that you may not be aware of. Perhaps you have raised a family who value your opinions and ideas. You may be in a supervisory position at work, guiding others with your expertise. Do your friends call you to talk things over because they admire your perceptions and solutions? You have a set of intuitive tools for living that are like the tools a carpenter uses for building. Some common positive traits many of us share are: intelligence, compassion, creativity, and courage.

To recover from compulsive behavior around money, you will have to believe that some of these inner powers are available to you, and retrieve them. These possibilities are like a water supply. You know it's there when you need it. You only need to turn on the faucet.

You keep a problem alive telling yourself that you don't know what to do. Here is a more in-depth list of the powerful inner qualities and traits you may call forth. You may want to copy it onto a small card or paper that you can keep in your wallet or hang up where it is easily seen. The next time you're telling yourself that your problem is hopeless and you don't know what to do, read through this list. Find the traits that you need to call forth from within to change your thoughts and your life.

It is fine to have three or four to work with. Use a bright colored marker or pen, and write the name of each quality on a separate card or piece of paper. Some people even make decorated posters. Hang these words up around your house on the refrigerator, the bathroom mirror, next to your bed, or even on the dashboard of your car. Each time you see the word you will be reminding yourself of what you can do to change things.

MY TOOLS

admiration	faith	positiveness
appreciation	freedom	power
attention	friendship	promptness
beauty	generosity	quiet
bliss	goodness	reality
brotherhood	goodwill	renewal
calm	gratitude	resoluteness
compassion	harmony	serenity
cooperation	humor	service

courage	infinity	silence
creativity	initiative	simplicity
daring	integration	tenacity
decisiveness	joy	truth
detachment	liberation	understanding
determination	light	universality
discipline	love	vitality
endurance	order	wholeness
energy	patience	will
enthusiasm	peace	wisdom
eternity	persistence	wonder

EXPERIENCE INNER WISDOM

We all perceive our world in three ways: through sight, through sound, and through touch or sensation. Although we use all our faculties every day, each of us seems to prefer one mode more than the others. I learn best from the printed word. I need to SEE what it is rather than be told about it. For people like me, reading self-help books, making lists, keeping personal journals, dealing with words I can refer to, work very effectively.

Auditory people prefer to hear what is going on. They would rather listen to something than watch it. The sounds are important to them. They may solve problems better by thinking about them in their heads rather than writing in a journal.

Kinesthetic people are the ones who *feel* the world. They are more in touch with physical sensations and emotions, and they often have strong feelings of intuition and sense things in different parts of their bodies. These are the people who say, "I had a feeling in my bones that something was wrong," while visual people say, "I see what you mean," and auditory people say, "I hear you loud and clear."

Your imagination is a vital resource and a marvelous tool for change. Many people think in symbols or colors rather than words. Often our schooling teaches us to discount our creative imagination. You can reclaim this tool now.

Symbols or pictures are equally valuable. When I am counseling, I may suddenly see a picture that I think relates to the other person. I recall a session in which I had a sudden image of a small crying baby. My client was a person recovering from both compulsive eating and spending. When I asked her how the idea of a small screaming child might relate to her, she told me that she remembered stealing food from the kitchen before she was three years old. Her mother would find shells from hard-boiled eggs or banana skins under her bed. She began to cry for the child who never felt loved and cared for. Eating and spending became the only ways she could give herself artificial comfort to replace the nurturing that was withheld by her parents.

I am going to suggest ways for you to retrieve your wonderful inner resources. Some activities that follow will be aimed for those of you who like to see and use words, while some will be about images or symbols. I will be asking you to use your creative imagination too. Try them all and open yourself to grow and change.

CONTACTING YOUR INNER KNOWER

There is a part of you that is wise and knowing. You may feel comfortable giving advice to your friends and family, but do you trust the advice you give yourself? The simplest way to meet and befriend your wisdom is to begin a correspondence. Exchange letters as if with a wise person from whom you want help. Write a brief letter inviting your wise adviser to guide you just as you would write to "Dear Abby." Pick someone you love or admire. It can be a real person like your grandmother, a favorite uncle, Shirley Maclaine, or Billy Graham or someone from history such as John F. Kennedy, Abraham Lincoln, Albert Schweitzer, or Socrates. I have known some people to write successfully to characters in fiction or mythology. One woman addressed her letter to the Goddess Athena.

Do your best to write a brief letter. Tell your wise counselor all about the problem. Be specific: who, what, when, where, why. Keep to the point. When you are through, reread what you have written and sign it. Take a fresh sheet of paper, put the date on top and write:

Dear ... (your name),

I received your letter and will gladly help you. You are a lovable person and deserve to find a solution to this problem ...

This is the answer from your inner guide. Since you do not know the answer, just let your pen do the talking. Keep writing about receiving help, and soon the words will come pouring out. Don't stop the flow. Write until you feel finished.

Read the letter you have just received. How will you know that it comes from a kind adviser and not from your inner critical sabotaging self? Ask yourself these easy questions.

1. Is the advice I have received *reasonable*?
2. Is it *loving* without being indulgent?
3. Is it *fair* and not harsh or punitive?
4. Am I willing to begin to take action to carry it out *now*?

The amazing thing about using this simple technique is that you can solve problems immediately. Sometimes there is nobody home to consult, or you aren't near a phone to call a friend or therapist. In teaching you how to write to Wisdom I am telling you that the answer is already within you. You know, but you don't know that you know. The more you practice letter writing, the more you will trust yourself and your wisdom.

For those people who prefer to visualize in pictures rather than words, sit in a private comfortable room for about ten minutes. Imagine yourself in a lovely place, the seashore, under a tree, on a mountain top, or in a special hidden spot. Think of the wisest, kindest person, living, dead, or fictional with whom you would like to talk things over. Invite him or her to join you. Tell your imaginary friend all about your troubles and hear what that person advises. Again, if it feels good, accept the advice, but if you don't like what the other offers, simply thank them and show them the door. Then invite another imaginary guide and try it again.

A computer programmer lets go of his problems at bedtime by imagining he is at work, seated at the computer keyboard. He types in his problem, briefly. Then he orders the computer to work on the answer and have it on his desk the next morning at 9 A.M. He turns off the imaginary computer terminal and drifts into sleep. Sure enough, as he sits at work the following day, at 9 A.M. the answer pops into his head!

An interesting variation on this theme is to write a dialogue with your problem. Write it as if it were a conversation between two characters in a play.

ME: What do I get out of letting you plague me every day?

PROBLEM: As long as I'm around, I keep you so busy you don't have time to see how unhappy you are with your spouse.

ME: How can I stop you from ruining my life?

PROBLEM: It's funny that you think I'm so strong and can run your life. You can pick up the reins any time you want.

Continue in this manner and see where it leads. You may discover something new and exciting about yourself.

SYMBOLS AS ANSWERS

Right-brained people enjoy solving problems in creative ways. Even if you are a logical, left-brained, intellectual, try some of these ideas. Buy some crayons or colored markers and draw a symbol or design that represents your urge to spend or shop. Think about what color or shape compulsion is to you. Draw a design that expresses your feelings after a binge. Hang both of them up and keep looking at them. Write down any new ideas that come to you.

Remember the list of inner resource qualities or traits? Find one that you want to focus on. Draw a symbol for it. Write the word underneath. You may choose love, patience, faith, persistence, or another.

If you have an important dream in which there is a unique character or animal, draw it. Kit had a dream about a huge mother dragon and a lost baby dragon. Even a week later, these images were clear, so I asked her to draw them. Then I instructed her to let each of these characters write her a short note telling her something about themselves or a message they had for her. She discovered that the lost dragon was her powerless self that felt small and helpless at work and in the adult world. The mother dragon represented immense creative energy and power. She felt extremely energized after this experience.

You don't have to be good at art to do this. Nobody will see it but you, and nobody is giving you a grade. You may have a picture in mind. If not, just take a crayon and start with the color that seems right. Then let yourself go on from there. Many of us as children played a game where we took a crayon and did a scribble on a paper. We turned the paper around until the scribble looked like something. Then we darkened the outline and finished the picture.

Gail wanted to change but felt powerless over her compulsion. She tried the scribble technique, and the picture looked like a bird. It said: "I am a bird about to fly, hesitant but excited to be free. I wish I were flying high, soaring and powerful. I need to know how easy it is to fly and believe it. I will soon be up in the clear blue."

USE YOUR CREATIVITY

One of my favorite games for contacting inner wisdom is so easy you can do it almost anywhere at anytime. I call it "The Magical A.T.M. Within." Most of us are familiar with the automatic teller machines available at our savings institutions. We go through three steps: first, punching in the proper information; second, waiting patiently while the machine does the work; and third, receiving our money or receipt.

To use the Magical A.T.M. Within, you go through the same procedures. First, formulate a question to which you truly have no answer or solution. You may want to jot the question down on paper. Next, get quiet, relax, and softly ask your question out loud. Then take a deep breath and let it out, saying "I don't know." Pretend you are standing at your local A.T.M. waiting confidently while the machine takes over. In a very few seconds the wondrous machines within will have processed your question and will give you the answer. Your answer will come as words in your head, perhaps a symbol or picture of someone or something, or a strong physical sensation. I have even received the answer as song lyrics!

Accept the very first thing that comes to you, no matter how absurd it may seem at first. Please don't censor it because you don't like it or are embarrassed by it. Assume that answer is correct. What would you want to ask next? Continue asking your inner A.T.M. questions until you feel satisfied. If you receive an answer that puzzles you, simply ask for clarification in your next transaction. Soon you may find that the answer comes as you are asking the question.

Have you ever played with a pendulum? Here is a surprising technique that you can use to find uniquely personal answers. Create a pendulum by using a locket on a chain, a key on a chain or simply hang a button on a piece of heavy thread. Sit comfortably holding the pendulum between your thumb and index finger, and let it dangle. The pendulum can move in these five ways:

1. Toward you and away from you
2. Across from right to left
3. Around in a clockwise circle
4. Around in a counter-clockwise circle
5. Stand perfectly still

Ask the pendulum to show you "YES" and notice which way it moves. Then ask for "NO" and "I DON'T KNOW." Ask questions aloud to which the answer will be yes or no. Then see what happens.

CREATE NEW RITUALS

Rituals are a vital part of every culture and each family. Rituals enrich our lives and often mark turning points. Our holidays are filled with activities that we enjoy. Religious and cultural observances mark the rites of passage from childhood to adult status. Graduation is a time to move forward educationally. Weddings celebrate the change of status. New Year's Eve is letting go of the old year and welcoming the new year. You can create exciting rites and ceremonies for just you as you move forward and free yourself of your compulsive behaviors.

When my children were in elementary school, we moved to a new neighborhood. Although the house was roomy and even had a swimming pool, we just couldn't get used to it. The house seemed permeated with the negative aura of the people who had previously lived in it. Finally, we decided to do something about the problem. We had a combination housewarming and exorcism party to take formal ownership of the house and rid ourselves of the "ghosts" of the past. Fortunately, I have a "magic wand" that I find helpful for such occasions. During the evening each guest was invited to wave the wand and bless our home. We lived in that house comfortably for the next ten years.

To celebrate her divorce, one of my friends had a party. Before the party ended she lit the barbecue in her backyard and ceremonially burned her marriage certificate to her now ex-husband. The idea of burning unwanted things to mark an end has an air of finality. I have assisted some of my clients who wish to leave old ideas and relationships behind by helping them to list each worn out belief on a piece of paper. We discuss them one at a time and solemnly burn them. After they are gone, the person makes a new list of more positive thoughts or beliefs that she chooses to live by. This technique also works when you write a letter to someone in your life expressing your resentment, hurt, or wish to be free. It is especially useful when the person is dead to burn the letter and watch the smoke rise, imagining the message is being transmitted.

WRITE A NEW SCRIPT

You don't have to fear change anymore. Earlier I told you that when we create a negative soap opera scenario we often seem to bring it to pass in our life. You can use your imagination and your sense of humor to envision a happy story. If you can't see yourself in the future being happy, solvent, free of compulsive urges, you can't achieve these goals. Spend as much time as you need to formulate a clear picture of the new life script you desire.

I create a scrapbook or collage when I want to make my vision of success concrete. This activity takes about an hour, perhaps two. Collect as many old magazines as you can. You also will need scissors, tape or glue, and either notebook paper or a large piece of tagboard. Take a moment to choose a theme for your work. I have made scrapbooks about prosperity, love, tranquility, health, a new home, and one to focus on overcoming my fear of flying.

It is best to do this activity alone, or if you are working with another person, don't talk. Enjoy yourself as you leaf through the magazines with your theme in mind. Search out pictures, words, and phrases that depict what you want. Keep at it until you have a good-sized collection. Then paste them onto the collage board or form a scrapbook.

Keep this creation handy. Hang the collage somewhere you can gaze at it and conjure up how wonderful you will feel when you have achieved your goal. Look through your scrapbook often. I once spent a marvelous afternoon creating a scrapbook of the perfect new house I wanted. Oddly, soon after, the scrapbook disappeared. I looked everywhere, but never found it. I then realized that I didn't think I was worthy of having a new home. I couldn't really accept thinking of myself in my dream house. About four years later, when I had a much better image, I did buy a new house. As we were packing to move, the scrapbook reappeared!

Looking at the pictures in your book will help you rehearse the good feelings you want. You also can have fun at a Success Party. All you have to do is to invite a few friends or acquaintances who are willing to experiment. Form a circle and ask each person to share some dream they have for the future. It must be stated in the positive, not "I want to stop binging," but "I want to be free of debt and own a beautiful home filled with lovely things."

Think of some way to denote the passing of time. You might set a timer and have everyone close their eyes for three minutes. If you have a magic wand, go around and wave it over each participant. Use your imagination! Tell your guests that when you give the signal it means that five or ten years have passed and they are in the future they predicted. Offer refreshments and ask your guests to mingle with each other talking as if they had everything they described. In other words, let them act as if they were successful.

You will be amazed at the fabulous energy you all will generate. This is a party your friends will long remember. I sometimes offer my friends a toy trophy or a certificate of success and we have a special awards ceremony before the party ends.

A common reason for spending or shopping is to amass *things* that may make you feel successful. Material possessions are only surface tokens and don't reflect your true inner worth. Most compulsive people have very low self-esteem. An easy way to begin to remedy this problem is to create a "Treasure Chest." Start by finding a sturdy or fancy container. You may have a cookie tin, a shoe box, a plastic sweater box or something else. Every time someone writes you a positive personal note or greeting card put it in your treasure box. Remember the handmade cards your children made for you in school or their kindergarten handprints? Put anything and everything that can remind you that you are indeed lovable and worthy into your container. When you feel depressed and low, or if you have had a money binge and are filled with self-hatred, take out your treasures and remind yourself that they represent the truth about you.

PERSONAL JOURNALS

Some people enjoy fantasy techniques and creative imagination exercises, but you may want to use more concrete and practical approaches for inner awareness. Putting your thoughts and feelings down on paper can help you relieve extreme tension and enable you to put things in perspective. There are many books about how to do psychological journal writing. You may already be writing. For some people, the easiest thing to do is buy a notebook and just start writing. Be sure to date each entry.

Your journal is your private possession. What you write is nobody else's business. Spelling doesn't count, nor does good grammar. The most important thing is to put down thoughts and feelings so you can work with them. Whether you write every day or every few days or just when you want to boil over, here is a plan that will help you. Reread what you have currently written and write the answer to these two questions at the bottom of the page:

1. What did I just discover from reading my journal?

2. What action can I take to change my circumstances? (Can I do something to improve my physical situation or relationship or can I change my attitude or self-talk?)

Other types of writing you may put in your journal are dialogues with people, living and dead; dialogues with memories, feelings, and binges. You also may write letters that you don't want to mail, but do want to get off your chest.

THE MESSAGE OF DREAMS

You also can keep a dream journal. Dreams come from within you. They are messages from you to you, but you may not know how to decode them. There are many excellent books about dream work for you to consult. Your therapist will work with you to understand dreams.

One kind of dream journal is simply to keep track of dreams by writing them down without trying to understand them. Write what you remember and make it as detailed as possible. After you have collected about twenty to thirty entries, read them through from start to finish. You may get the message immediately.

When I was working to overcome my codependency tendencies and my compulsive activities with food and spending, I had a series of dreams that seemed very silly. I kept dreaming about Ladies' Rooms. Sometimes I was in a department store and had to find the Ladies Room, other times it was in a house or school or other setting. The words that always went with the dream were "Ladies Room," not toilet or bathroom. The dreams stayed in my mind and bothered me. They didn't happen every night, but were frequent enough for me to see that there was some pattern. I started to write them down and keep them. Finally, I read a month's worth of dreams.

Much to my delight, I discovered that the words "Ladies Room" symbolized finding my new place in the world as a capable and talented woman (lady) who can take care of myself financially. The dreams were reassuring me that I was succeeding.

Besides journal writing, dream writing, and self exploration through writing it is important to honor your other creative expressions. You may enjoy writing poetry or songs. I envy people who can write stories. Let yourself go. Fiction is often autobiographical. Create a new story of how you want life to be. Fill it with sunshine and love.

RELEASE STRESS

Meditation and guided fantasy techniques can give you a respite from worry and fear. You can enjoy a feeling of peace and calm while you allow your unconscious to do the work. You can use these suggestions for a time-out, to allow time for healing physical stress, or to allow time to receive guidance.

One simple fantasy is to imagine yourself in a quiet, beautiful, safe place. Some people recall actual scenes from nature, others create a private place that is completely imaginary. You can even create a thick wall around your safe place to make sure of privacy. Concentrate on the beauty of your surroundings. Let down your guard and float in relaxation. Music in the background often enhances the mood.

There are times I truly want to relax but can't let go completely. A trick I use at these times is to put on quiet music and imagine myself holding a huge bunch of brilliantly colored balloons. Each balloon has writing on it. I take one balloon at a time and notice that the writing tells me of a situation or relationship that is worrying or frustrating me. I read the words and let go of the balloon. As I watch it soar into the blue I let go of my worry . . . for now. I take my time to make sure that I have let go of every concern. Soon the sky is filled with a bouquet of color and I feel wonderful as I watch them disappear.

An unusual fantasy is the trip down "Memory Lane." Sit comfortably and close your eyes. Let your thoughts take you back through your life as you relive the *happiest* moments. Make sure you look only for positive memories. Remember friends from your childhood, parties, pets, trips, beautiful scenery, triumphs, secret joys, and even smells and tastes. Feel free to travel back and forth in time savoring each memory. Take as long as you like.

The "Magical Mystery Tour" is a surprise fantasy trip. Choose a lyrical piece of music and let it take you somewhere. You may know where you want to go or can pretend to see a door and go through it to somewhere that pleases you. In your imaginary travels you may find some answers to your problems. Music has great power to evoke emotion. Be sure to select pieces that can relax and uplift.

I have been told that the genius Mozart used to have his wife read aloud to him from a novel while he composed. He said it distracted him so he could let the music flow through him. When you focus on your limitations, doubts, and fears, you close the channel to your divine "music." Let go and let your cares float away like little toy boats gliding down the stream. As you relax, many insights can come into your awareness. Stop trying so hard to make things happen!

FAITH, YOUR INVISIBLE STRENGTH

One reason anonymous programs have been so successful is that the Twelve Steps are a program of spiritual recovery. You can be spiritual even if you are not religious. Many of my clients have turned away from the religion of their youth and feel guilty about it. A belief in any loving, divine power greater than yourself is the greatest tool you have.

I once knew a wonderful and charismatic minister who would listen patiently to the outpourings of his parishioners sufferings. After the final "ain't it awful and there's nothing I can do about it," he would smile and gently say, "Don't you have an invisible means of support?" He knew that each person was a channel, but most of us block that channel with our limited negative thinking, what Alcoholics Anonymous refers to as "stinkin' thinkin'." As you explore the spiritual dimension, you will find that you can use this power to alter your situation and your problems.

Many people whose faith is strong practice prayer and meditation to achieve a conscious contact with their Higher Power. Yet each of us can be a divine channel for good.

There is a wonderful story often told in Alcoholics Anonymous about two prospectors in the Yukon who were arguing over the existence of God. One maintains that there is a God, while the other says he has proof that there is no God. "How can you prove there is no God?" "Well," says the doubter, "I was out prospecting and got lost in a blizzard. The snow erased my trail. I thought I was a goner. I got down on my knees and prayed, 'God, if there is a God, please help me now!'" "But you are here," said the believer, "That proves there is a God." "Naw," said the doubter, "Some damn Eskimo came and showed me the way home."

Eskimos are people who appear in your life and give you information or opportunities that then change your life. In other words, their intervention leads you to a new place in your life. You never know when an Eskimo will pop up.

Until I was thirty-five I hovered between being an atheist and an agnostic. After a few years in a Twelve-Step program, I discovered my Higher Power, but I was definitely anti organized religion. I was practicing my brand of spirituality when a friend gave me the phone number of a dial-a-prayer that turned out to be wonderful. When my day wasn't going well, I could pick up the phone and receive incredible help in just a minute. Whoever the minister was, he seemed to be talking directly to me in words that made sense. The message was brief with no mention of the church or the name of the minister.

About six months later I signed up for a weekend Twelve-Step retreat led by a minister. The workshop was inspiring. I experienced some major breakthroughs under the guidance of this excellent teacher. By Sunday I was determined to find out where the minister's church was. I told myself that even if I had to drive an hour, I wanted what he had. I finally got up the nerve to ask him, as the weekend ended. Much to my delight I discovered that his church was only twenty minutes away, and that his was the voice of my favorite dial-a-prayer! Studying with him was a great joy of my life. He was one of my favorite Eskimos.

A phrase you hear often in the anonymous program is "turn it over." That means to trust your faith and remember that you aren't God and can't control everyone or everything. Spending binges can be a way to get even with someone in your life, especially when that someone isn't doing what you want, the way you want, when you want it.

One easy way to release your frustration or anxiety about another is to give that person to God. I suggest that you picture him or her surrounded with light. As you let go of your worry or concern, tell yourself that this person is being taken care of by someone infinitely more powerful and loving. Or write a letter to his guardian anger asking the angel to watch over him.

What about you? Surround yourself with light and put yourself in the hands of your spiritual power. In times of enormous stress I have found some of these affirmations helped me gain my perspective:

Divine loving action is now taking place.
Divine love is now present in this situation.
I deserve the very best, *now*.
I now forgive myself and approve of myself.
I am always in my right place.
If not this, something better.

HOW TO FORGIVE

Recently a woman in one of my classes reported that her mother, who had physically and emotionally abused her throughout her childhood, had called to ask her daughter's forgiveness. My student announced that as an active member of a church she believed in forgiveness, so why was she still angry and resentful?

Although forgiveness is a tool to help you heal the emotional wounds that still plague you, you cannot forgive until you are ready. The adult woman believed in forgiveness, but the small child within, who had to endure multiple beatings and other cruelties, couldn't imagine forgiving the wicked mother. You cannot truly be free of anger and resentment until you nurture your wounded child within. That child was hurt and shamed by many unhappy experiences where nobody seemed to honor her needs or wanted to know about her fears.

It is usually the inner child who decides to go on a spree. That "needy greedy" part of you that hasn't been loved will look for an artificial feel-good when it feels deprived of closeness, respect, love, approval, or power. John Bradshaw's books, workshops, and television talks are showing millions the way to reclaim and attend to the child we all once were.

When you are ready to begin forgiving those who have caused you pain, you may want to write down the name of the person and what they did to you. Ask yourself if you can let go of that old hurt. If you can, you may want to simply announce that you are free of the old anger and now free the other person to live his or her life happily. It may be easier if you write that person a letter explaining what happened and that you are now letting go of your grudge. You don't mail the letter. A therapist, sponsor, or clergyman can help you facilitate this work.

After my divorce I was still consumed with anger toward my ex-husband because his compulsive spending had bankrupted us. He rarely paid child support, and I found myself struggling to support our children and make a new life for myself. When I was willing to accept responsibility for my actions in playing along as a "binge-buddy" and codebtor, I finally could let go of my expectations of him. A week after the change in my attitude, he called and told me that his life was improving dramatically. I laughed as I shared that I had recently released my anger toward him. He replied, "Your hold on me was very great." As part of my "let go" I stopped aggravating over the lack of child support. And he started to pay more regularly after that.

Compulsive people are highly self-critical. I like to remind them that in our country murderers often get out of jail in less than seven years, but bingers condemn themselves to a life imprisonment of guilt and shame. Now is the time to forgive yourself. I believe that at every moment of our life we are doing the best we can. If we could do better we would do better.

What offenses are you still holding yourself responsible for? What is the worst thing you have ever done to yourself or to others? Are you willing to write a complete list of your misdemeanors? I know that you are harder on yourself than anyone in the world could be. If this list belonged to the person you love most in the world, what would you want to tell that person? See if you can read each item on your list out loud to yourself and say, "I forgive me."

As you consider the way your compulsive acting out has harmed yourself and others, you may decide to take action to make amends and to make yourself responsible for paying debts. It is time to stop holding onto self-hatred and make a new plan.

MEDITATION THAT WORKS

People who practice meditation report excellent results. They improve both their physical and mental health. The first time someone suggested that I meditate I laughed at her. I couldn't imagine sitting in a chair and doing nothing! In those days I hadn't yet realized that keeping busy was my way of not feeling my feelings. I couldn't afford to be still long enough for my rage to surface.

Another excuse I used was that I didn't know how and might do it wrong. Meditation is quieting the mind. There are may ways to meditate. Joggers and runners often go into a meditative state, and they are in motion. The important idea about meditation is to stay in the now-moment. Your mind will constantly wander. See if you can find a way to stay focused. Many people use mantras, phrases or sounds they repeat like *Ohm*. You can choose a favorite phrase from a prayer or a word of inspiration like *peace, love*, or *health*. As you prevent your thoughts from dwelling on the negative and spend a few minutes thinking in a positive way, you will feel renewed and refreshed. New thoughts and ideas will flow into your mind.

One famous psychiatrist put glow-in-the-dark stars on the ceiling of his office. While his patients lay on the couch he would darken the room, and they would see the stars shine. In this cosmic setting he would then ask the patient, "How will all this matter in a hundred years?" Practicing meditation helps you put things in a new perspective. As you let go of mind-

chatter, you can become more relaxed and less stressed.

THE POWER OF THE CREATIVE UNCONSCIOUS

In this book I am teaching you to stop feeling like
a victim in life. You have all the power you need to
solve your problem, create a happy new life-plan, and
stick to it. You do need support as you work on
yourself. Psychotherapy, classes, groups, self-help organizations, and other training will allow you to find
the strength within. There is a power within you. I
often call it inner wisdom or your creative unconscious.
It is the part of you that knows what to do and how to
do it.

You will not retrieve your power unless you believe
that you have the power to help yourself. Although
groups, classes, and individual counseling will ease
change, the healing comes through you. The more you
give yourself opportunities to learn how to get in touch
with the resources within, your inner wisdom or
creative unconscious, the easier it will become to know
what to do and how to do it.

Under hypnosis you can mentally return to a
moment in childhood. You could describe in great
detail the activities, the words, and the feelings you
have experienced. Every experience you've ever lived
is stored somewhere within. Think of your unconscious
as a large library filled with millions of recorded
moments. Be confident that by using the methods I

have described, you can have access to all that you need. The raw materials for success are waiting for you. Only you can know when to act and how to put it all together.

HOW TO GET STARTED

If you aren't ready to work the STOP-LOOK-LISTEN plan today you can become ready. Begin with a letter to your wise advisor asking how to help yourself take the first step. Or call on your "cosmic teller." If you only take one step toward positive change it will lead to the next and the next.

Remember that working this plan can change your life. If you find yourself resisting, think about why you want to hang on to your problem. Only when you are sick-and-tired of being sick-and-tired will you change. In my life I have discovered that when the pain of what I'm doing outweighs the pleasure I get from doing it, I change.

You may not want to wait until the consequences of spending or debting produces overwhelming pain in your life. If you are still wary, let me assure you that you do not need to give up having nice things or going places because you give up abusing spending. Change doesn't have to hurt; fighting change hurts more.

The program I have described in this book is simple although it is not easy. I am asking you for a commitment to become willing to be *conscious*, to observe your behaviors and take responsibility for how you spend or debt. Remember, a binge is a signal of a life out of balance. It is saying, "OUCH!"

Living consciously means that you stop lying to yourself and feel your feelings. The STOP-LOOK-LISTEN program teaches you to listen to your thoughts and beliefs. Keep viewing your behavior, your feelings and your thoughts as you ask yourself, "Is this adding to my life or causing me pain?" If it harms you, why hang on to it? Use your newfound skills; contact your inner adviser; find new solutions. The result is that you will learn to know and trust in yourself as a lovable and capable human being, one who deserves the very best. You are the only one who can decide when you want to trade your misery for a life free of the bondage of compulsive spending and debting.

LOOSE CHANGE

10

GETTING OUTSIDE HELP

People have sought my help in overcoming addictive and compulsive problems—alcoholism, drug abuse, eating disorders, codependency—and although many of these clients also suffered from compulsive spending or debting, they rarely touched on the problem until well into our work together. Until recently our population considered money abuse an annoying bad habit and didn't see the relationship to other addictions.

Compulsive spenders, and those who unconsciously are driven to get rid of their money by excessive debting, need to work to overcome depression, relationship difficulties, fear, or anxiety. These are the underlying problems. Yet, unless they address their specific negative behaviors with money and credit these habits will not disappear by themselves.

Many therapists, like others in our culture, tend to ignore excessive spending and debting as a significant part of a client's life. There are very few psychotherapists who are knowledgeable about treating spending disorders. Many who specialize in addictive behaviors tend to discount spending and debting as less important than alcohol or drugs. Yet, many people who become sober as members of Twelve-Step programs become aware that they have transferred their urge for pleasure from a substance—alcohol, food, or drugs—to a behavior: spending.

Compulsive spending or debting is a sign of other unresolved issues or feelings. Finding a therapist who understands the problems related to addictive or compulsive acts is important. Therapy must provide both behavior modification and new tools for resolving life issues.

As you seek professional help for compulsive spending you will come across different types of therapy. The most common type is talk therapy, where you and the counselor sit together and talk about your problem. There are different kinds of talk therapy too. Some therapists work from an analytical framework, while cognitive therapy, transactional analysis, and rational emotive therapy create new educational experiences. You will learn to make healthier choices, change your attitude toward life, and create new behaviors.

Body-work therapies are also popular. You may have heard of Rolfing, Bio-energetics, or Neo-Richian therapies. Body-work therapists will touch you or massage you in ways that release locked-in energies imprisoned in the body. As the flow of energy is unblocked, feelings and memories emerge. You can improve your posture and body tone at the same time you explore the unconscious.

A third type of psychotherapy is offered through creative processes. This therapy is experiential, involving activities to enable you to bypass conscious resistance so you can access your unconscious. You will find new awarenesses and solutions. Art therapy, music therapy, dance therapy, guided imagery, dream analysis, and hypnosis can all be considered creative therapies.

In each of these processes you will be experiencing right brain activity. We think that the right brain is the seat of intuition and creativity, while the left brain relates to words, logical thinking, and mathematics. Creative therapies are not meant for artists and musicians, but for everyone, even those who consider themselves unable to draw or dance gracefully. They are not really about art or music, but about symbolism and new ways to understand yourself.

GROUP THERAPY

Although you will benefit enormously from individual counseling, you may find that a group therapy experience offers another powerful growth opportunity. When people share their feelings and problems, the work results in understandings and changes not always possible with other approaches. Again, there are many choices. Support groups are often leaderless, whereas group therapy is conducted by a trained professional. Nonprofessional self-help groups such as Debtors Anonymous will bring you into contact with others like you.

The best thing about the group experience is that you will soon discover that you are not the only person in the world to feel the way you do or behave as you do. Identification with others leads you out of your isolation. Another plus is that you can receive feedback about how other people see you or react to you. As you change, the group can support you and help you through the rough times and the moments when you risk new behaviors.

Being a member of a group can be an inspirational experience as you benefit from the success of other members who are freeing themselves from compulsive behaviors. Many members of Debtors Anonymous also belong to Alcoholics Anonymous and Overeaters Anonymous.

Self-help groups are springing up everywhere to address other related problems. Some organizations that you may want to know about are: Al-Anon, Codependents Anonymous, and Adult Children of Alcoholics (and Trauma). Emotional Health Anonymous is a Twelve-Step group that helps people deal with out-of-control emotions. Recovery is not a Twelve-Step organization. Recovery has been in existence for many years helping people deal with debilitating emotional problems, especially depression. Since most of these groups are nonprofit, they are usually free, so there is little reason not to get help.

WHICH THERAPY WORKS BEST?

Dr. Stanton Peele recommends that, "the best thing people can do to solve or prevent addiction is to learn to control their destinies, to find social and work rewards, and to minimize—or at least to bring within controllable limits—stress and fear." In his book, *Diseasing of America*, Dr. Peele discusses people who have improved their lives and given up addictive behaviors without therapy. He suggests that effective therapy would produce these same results:

1. To increase desire for change.
2. To help the client learn to accept and cope with negative emotions and experiences.
3. To develop life resources so that change may take place at work, at home and within.
4. To enable the client to view the compulsive behavior as undesirable.
5. To help the client live an effective life in keeping with his values.

To let go of compulsive urges you must rethink these questions:

- Who am I?
- What is good for me?
- How do I want my life to be?
- What lifestyle changes are necessary?

Loose Change

The most successful types of therapy are: behavior modification, cognitive therapy, marital and family therapy, social skills training, and stress management.

Behavior modification involves self watching. Many compulsive people prefer to see themselves as power-less over their behavior and want others to police them or fix them. Self-control is a series of conscious choices while compulsion is a series of choices too, only they are choices you resist acknowledging. Behavior modification training helps you to become responsible for your choices. You learn from each choice you make. As you become more conscious of your urges and cravings you will make more appropriate choices. In behavior modification, a slip is just an opportunity for change, it isn't a relapse.

Cognitive therapy will teach you to question your negative thoughts and beliefs and learn to create alternative ways of thinking that can create a new way of acting. If you think you can control your spending, you can. Many studies in the field of alcoholism have proved that people who think of themselves as al-coholic are more likely to drink excessively when they drink, even when they actually are not drinking alcohol but only *believe* they are. I have a poster that says, "If you think you can . . . or you think you can't . . . you are right."

The family systems approach to marital and family counseling views the relationship as greater than the sum of its parts. This kind of counseling examines the interactions between the family members instead of focusing on one person as the sick one. Family systems therapy helps everyone in the family learn new and positive techniques for dealing with family stress and communication issues.

Social skills that compulsive people need are mainly assertiveness training and communication improvement so they can express their feelings clearly and directly and ask for what they want. These skills can help with personal relationships and work-related problems that may arise with co-workers or supervisors. Remember, a binge is usually saying, "Ain't it awful, and there's nothing I can do about it!" Assertiveness training often restores a sense of effectiveness in dealing with difficult people.

Stress management is especially important for everyone. When you learn ways to relax you can think about your problems from a new point of view. You can figure out options and consider alternatives other than binging. Stress management will improve mental health and boost physical well-being.

THE ROLE OF A THERAPIST

You may never have gone to a therapist before, and you may be very apprehensive. Therapists are not mechanics who fix you the way a car mechanic fixes a flat tire. The therapist doesn't make something happen to you. Therapy is more like a journey you make together. You are the traveler, and your counselor is the guide. He or she knows the trail and is alert for the pitfalls along the way. As long as you keep trudging you will reach your destination.

A mental health professional has been trained to teach you new skills so you can transform your difficulties and increase your happiness and effectiveness. Therapists don't give advice! Beware of someone who thinks for you or demands that you act a certain way. A therapist who rescues you keeps you from feeling the pain of your mistakes and takes away your opportunity to find personal solutions by exploring your thoughts, feelings and perceptions. Each therapist has a unique style. Find the person you feel in tune with.

When I was nine I went to summer camp and learned how to swim. On the day I was ready to graduate from the shallow pool to deep water, they put a rope around my waist and stood me at the edge of the dock. The counselor told me that it was okay to jump. She knew that I knew how to swim and that I wouldn't drown, though I wasn't so sure. She reminded me that she was holding the rope and wouldn't let anything bad happen to me.

I tell my clients that story and let them know that I am holding their rope. Whatever new behavior or risk they are ready for, we can discuss it and evaluate it step-by-step. They have to take the plunge in their world to communicate in a new way, say no when they've never said it before, break up relationships, or look for new jobs. I can't do it for them; I can only reassure them that I know they have the skills and won't drown.

One important thing I can do for clients is to offer unconditional acceptance. My clients are so down on themselves that they have a difficult time understanding that their spending behavior is merely an inadequate solution to their other life problems. As they stop judging themselves they can begin to look for other helpful resources, learn new skills, and practice stress reduction

I have described many therapeutic alternatives for you. Remember that besides private counseling there are low-cost clinics that offer help. Do not work with anyone you can't trust. When you have to hold back information or feel ashamed to share with your therapist, you won't benefit from your sessions. There are many health professionals, just as there are many plumbers, doctors, and lawyers. You have a right to shop for the person you will be paying for the best service. We tend to put doctors and therapists on a pedestal in our culture. They are just people, human and imperfect just like you.

As a lay person, you have little information or experience to give you a sound basis for making the right choice. Some therapists belong to an analytical tradition while others are transpersonal and focus on both spiritual and emotional aspects of your being. As a client you will receive treatment according to the therapist's preference and training, but it may not be what will help you overcome your specific problem.

Most psychotherapists are trained like general practitioners to deal with a little bit of every type of problem. Some of these people continue to attend workshops and classes about many topics, but they don't go deeply into certain areas. If they don't keep up with the literature or see many cases, they may not have the expertise you need. I urge you to seek someone whose practice is devoted more than fifty percent of the time to treating addiction or compulsion. You can choose from psychiatrists, psychologists, social workers, marriage and family therapists, or pastoral counselors.

Ask whether your therapist works only from a Twelve-Step recovery approach, is anti-Twelve-Step, or can work with you from a varied or neutral point of view. If you are already a member of an anonymous organization, you will feel best working with someone who can understand your program of recovery and help you use it to overcome spending or debting.

It is not necessary to have recovered from the same problem as a client to be a good therapist. Still, some clients feel more comfortable working with someone who has recovered from a compulsive behavior. You can decide if this is important to you.

Here are some guidelines to help you choose:

1. The therapist specializes in addictive and compulsive disorders.
2. The therapist continues to read in the field of specialization and goes to training, workshops and conferences for continued education.

3. The therapist admits limitations and doesn't pretend to know things he or she doesn't know.
4. The therapist says things that make sense to you.
5. The therapist answers your direct questions.
6. The therapist is willing to see significant people in your life as part of your recovery process.
7. The therapist acts as your consultant rather than as a judgmental parent.

When my daughter was a teenager we decided to go for family counseling. We chose a prestigious psychologist with many letters after his name and an impressive reputation. After two sessions we realized that none of us wanted to go back. We didn't feel heard, understood, or respected. We didn't like the man at all! About a year after we changed therapists I bumped into a former acquaintance. She seemed much happier than I'd ever seen her. She told me that it was a result of psychotherapy. She went to a fabulous person who had helped her revolutionize her life. It turned out to be the same man with whom my family had felt uncomfortable.

Only you will know if you are comfortable with your therapist. You may enjoy being with a dynamo or a reserved, quiet, person. Think about whether you could share intimate facts better with a male or female. You have chosen wisely if you begin to see signs of change in your mood or your behavior after a short time. The therapy office is a private place to air your feelings and resolve problems in a safe environment. If you think this is your next step, take action now and you will have a happier future.

11

PAST LIVES
PRESENT PROBLEMS

 I have discovered that besides teaching my clients behavior modification techniques, cognitive techniques, and relaxation or self-hypnosis, many compulsive people benefit from a type of guided imagery I label *Past Life Allegory*. An allegory is a symbolic narrative.

Past life therapy is a technique for searching out lifetimes that were traumatic or emotionally charged to promote insight into the present situation or relationship. By reliving the past life story in a dramatic way, a healing of the present problem is possible. When a person allows himself to create a story about someone in his past life, even himself, a drama unfolds that mirrors many central issues or fears belonging to this lifetime.

It is unnecessary to question the validity of past lives. This imagery technique simply allows your Creative Unconscious to provide a meaningful story, giving you information about yourself that you need to know.

Past life allegories are usually vivid recreations that resemble an historical movie. Sometimes there is a glimpse of an important moment. At other times, the person gets in touch with a lifetime that seems to reflect a single theme such as loneliness, failure, loss of love, or abandonment. Often these are the feelings that trigger spending binges.

I advise my client to pretend that he is an understudy for the star of a play, and the star has taken ill in the middle of Act Two. The person must go on in the middle of the play but will know all the lines and will be aware of what has already occurred in Act One. The difference between a guided fantasy and a past life allegory is that the allegory seems prewritten just like a play or a video cassette. The understudy merely continues the plot as written. In a guided fantasy, the imager can change the elements or action of the story at will to create or change the experience or mood.

During the session, while the conscious mind is providing the dialogue, the unconscious is revealing the major conflicts that are unresolved and are causing difficulties in your present life. The historical setting will help you put these ideas and feelings at arm's length to understand them more clearly. Past life experiences must be handled carefully because some incidents in the story can be powerful or frightening. This is definitely a therapeutic tool, not a parlor game. I want to caution you to do it only with someone who is trained to guide you and help you understand the significance of your experience.

IT WAS ALL YOUR FAULT

I have already described that after I stopped eating at my ex-husband I began to spend at him. Although we divorced, my anger toward him would not abate. A few years later I underwent past life therapy and had an experience as an English youth named Jeremy who was sent to an insane asylum because his family mistook his epilepsy for insanity. This happened in the 1700s.

As I relaxed into the story, I became aware of the stench of unwashed bodies and filthy excrement as I felt myself sprawled on my back in dirty, bug-infested straw. I was among a group of people who had been herded into a large area like a prison cell. I felt horribly alone and frightened. The idea of living out my life in this disgusting prison was unthinkable. Death was the only solution. "I want to die," I decided.

The guard was an insensitive brute who treated the inmates as if we were animals. He put down a bucket of putrid slop for the "loonies" to scoop up. There was dead vermin floating in it. As Jeremy, I felt the nausea rise up, thinking that I would starve if I didn't eat it. My only recourse was to taunt the sadistic jailor until he killed me. That's what I did as Jeremy. I made the guard so angry that he mauled me, throwing my body against the wall, breaking my arms and legs and pounding me until all life had gone from my body.

Jeremy's life was quite a surprise for me. I was hoping to find a past life to vindicate me and allow me to continue my anger toward my ex-husband. Instead, although I discovered that the guard was my ex-husband, I had to recognize that there were times in my marriage that, like Jeremy, I too had "asked for it" by acting critical and sarcastic. Like Jeremy I felt like a victim, but instead of leaving the marriage, I martyred myself, complaining about how awful things were . . . but staying, nonetheless.

After my divorce I became a self-debtor, living on food stamps and Aid For Dependent Children as a way of getting back at him and at the same time waiting for him to make up to me for making our married years so difficult.

Reliving this past life forced me to take responsibility for my part in both choosing the man I married and for choosing to stay in that terrible relationship. After this session I could no longer justify my rage. I had to get on with my life and support myself.

BORN TO FAIL

Eleanor, the fiftyish woman I described in chapter two, who was recovering from alcoholism, compulsive eating, and spending and debting, recalled a past life as a businessman named Joseph who lived in New

England in the 1800s. He and his brother were in the import business at a time when there were sailing ships and many disasters. Joseph's brother could take risks and succeed, but when he died in a carriage accident, Joseph became bitter. "I should have taken better care of him. It's my fault," thought Joseph. Then he vowed to take care of his brother's family and be strong.

But Joseph wasn't a very good businessman. He ordered one of the sea captains to sail on a doomed voyage. His poor judgment caused the business to fail. "I knew I was wrong when I gave the order, but in my arrogance I was too stubborn to back down. Everything is gone. I deserved it." Afterward, Joseph committed suicide.

Eleanor labeled this life "Born To Be A Failure." Although she came from a family of wealth, in the end she too had squandered her money. When Eleanor binged, she often bought three or four of the same item, but gave them as gifts to others and kept herself poor.

A CLASS STRUGGLE

I characterized Cora as a "Needy Greedy Child" in a previous chapter. Cora's spending often had to do with a class struggle. She originally came from a poor family and spent money to "pass as middle class." Her past life allegory parallels the theme of one woman's struggle to compete in a man's world. In that lifetime

Loose Change

Cora found herself in the 1800s as a wealthy widow in her forties who had started a jewelry business. She had spent most of her money on inventory and was proud of her shop.

The men in the family were embarrassed by her because she wouldn't "stay in her place" and was too independent for a rich woman of that class. They therefore conspired to have the shop burned down. Everything was lost. Cora was helpless after that, conceding that she shouldn't have stepped out of her role. She knew it wasn't her fault, but felt guilty anyway.

"There's nothing for me to do but live like other women and do boring things," she said. The woman lived a life of helplessness and boredom until she died. When she knew her place and stayed in it, her family gathered around her, but she remained embittered to the end. She characterized her life by saying,"I never got to do anything productive again. I didn't do anything with my life!"

Today Cora is a person who is very resourceful at not keeping her money. She manages to spend it in buying binges or lends it to people who won't pay her back. She is still fighting to become and stay an independent woman with good business sense. Parenthetically, Cora also confided in me that she has a very hard time hanging on to her jewelry. She either loses it or has been burglarized of her jewels.

BORN TO SPEND

You may recall that I labeled Lupe as indulgent due to her insatiable urge to buy clothing. She abuses her credit cards and enjoys owning property. A house means self-worth to Lupe. In her past life allegory Lupe took the part of a very independent young woman who lived in the 1920s and liked to dress well. She worked hard at her job. One day the boss offered to marry her. She knew that he was a good man who would take care of her, but she didn't love him. She turned him down and continued to work at a job she felt was beneath her. Eventually she did better and better. "I feel secure about money and can do what I want. I feel in control of my life. I don't feel obligated toward someone else."

As time went on the woman became manager of a successful department in a high-class store. She never married, but didn't feel desolate because she had made a success of herself. Lupe identified with that woman as she told me, "I feel wonderful in a department store. It is as if I'm on drugs. I feel depressed if there's something I want and I can't buy it." The woman in the past life didn't have to spend money to make herself feel good and attractive. Lupe had to have *things* to make herself feel attractive. She is obsessed with taking care of herself and becoming independent. At times she has worked at two high-paying jobs simultaneously.

Reexperiencing lifetimes that were traumatic or emotionally charged can promote insight by understanding the lessons of that lifetime. By reliving the past life story in all its intensity, a healing release of the present problem takes place. Whether it really happened or not, the experience of the past life regression leads to insights and change.

12

ADVICE TO FAMILY AND FRIENDS

You may be reading this chapter because there is someone in your life who is spending or debting compulsively, and you feel frustrated and angry with them. You don't understand why they do what they do, and you can't understand why they can't just use a little more willpower. Perhaps you have tried bribery, threats, punishment, rewards, pleading, or trickery, to no avail. You may have decided to simply ignore the problem and hope it will go away in time.

Compulsive spenders or debtors often have unhappy or dysfunctional relationships. You may be part of one of these. Usually the compulsive spender considers herself a victim of circumstances. She may have led you into acting the role of either her persecutor or her rescuer. When you accept the challenge to change the one with the problem by acting like an authority and policing her behavior, setting up punishments or simply yelling at her or belittling her, you will be the loser because the victim will rebel against your power play.

Sometimes the person who acts like the parent keeping the child in line can make the spender or debtor "shape up" temporarily, but she will feel resentment toward you and will find ways, sometimes very passively, to go against your wishes.

Although you may find it easy to live within your means and not abuse your credit cards, your friend or loved one doesn't know how yet. He feels great self hatred every time he tries and fails. When you put him down with insults or look disapprovingly or disappointedly at him, he feels even worse. Nothing you can say or do will make him feel worse than his inner critic is already doing.

Acting parental and critical toward the compulsive spender doesn't work. Rescuing isn't effective either. What you consider as kind or loving can really be considered rescue. Don't do for the other what he can do for himself, if he wants to. When you try to protect the other so he doesn't encounter temptation or conflict, you are merely postponing things. Stop backing down and refraining from saying or doing things you are afraid will upset him.

Many compulsive people seek out others who will take care of them. Once the relationship is in full swing the spender begins to alternate between loving and hating the rescuer. He will feel happy at being free of the responsibilities for his behavior, knowing someone else is there to pick up the pieces or pay bills that are past due. But eventually the victim will think the rescuer is superior and will grow to resent being cared for.

When my ex-husband and I were in terrible financial straits my mother always came to our rescue. She didn't lend us money; she gave us money. We could remain victims because we didn't have to become responsible and figure out how to pay her back. Then I noticed that her gifts also made me feel extremely inadequate. Her rescues made me doubt my ability and power to act like an adult in the financial arena of my world.

Gary's wife Gail put him on an allowance. At first he was delighted that she was in charge. Eventually he began to borrow money from friends to pay for things when his allowance ran out. Soon he started using the credit card he had put aside. He felt like a bad little boy doing a naughty thing behind mommy's back. Instead of learning to control his urges, he waited for his wife to do it for him.

Codependents or enablers are those who seek relationships in which they see themselves as nurturing or saving someone. Like alcoholics, compulsive debtors frequently are attracted to these helper types. After a while, however, the helper may become angry because the debtor isn't changing, or the debtor will feel angry because he has to keep striving to get better to feel loved. Resentment can trigger spending sprees that are temper tantrums toward the helping angel. Many of these helping angels have other compulsive problems themselves. Their resentment toward the spender can trigger eating or drinking binges.

The relationship between the victim and rescuer may run into difficulties as the victim starts to recover and doesn't need to be saved. What does a rescuer do when there is no victim?

Sandy, a client who had originally started treatment for her problem with compulsive overeating, realized that she had rescued her husband, a compulsive debtor, for nine years. Her salary paid the mortgage. Through the years she had liquidated all the savings she had amassed before her marriage to keep the bill collectors happy. When things got rough she borrowed money from her parents. As an enabler, she was very much a part of her husband's problem. One day I asked her, "What would you do if you were married to an adequate man?" In that moment Sandy realized that if she was married to a man with no money compulsions she would feel unimportant. She might not be "needed." While life was a soap opera in which she didn't know how they would get out of each scrape, it seemed exciting. She didn't have time to stop and feel her feelings. She just ate to suppress them. Martyrdom had become her way of life. She enjoyed hearing her friends and family saying, "How can you live with him? You are wonderful for putting up with it."

Sandy finally got tired of putting up with it and divorced her husband. But she wasn't free of her need to rescue. She soon took up with a self-denying man who hadn't held a job in two years. Sandy rose to the bait and took him under her wing. It took two more years of psychotherapy for her to let go of that relationship. She could then seek out men who were responsible adults, free of money compulsions who didn't need rescuing.

Persecutors are people who inflict guilt trips on the spender/debtor by making them responsible for the persecutor's well-being. This was the situation with Frank, whose mother was in her eighties and sickly but who bailed him out with all her savings. Whenever Frank did something his mother disapproved of, his mother would say, "You'll be the death of me." This didn't stop Frank, but it made him more guilty.

Loretta's husband would assault his spendthrift wife with, "If you really loved me, you would stop getting us into debt." No amount of scare or threat will deter compulsive spenders. They aren't doing it to hurt you, although if they know that it bothers you it becomes a tempting way of manipulating or punishing you.

A problem with being a policeman is that you must constantly judge the other. In truth, the words "good" and "bad" are unproductive, tending to keep the spender in a state of guilt and fear. The result is that the compulsive person will maintain even more secrecy, and that will increase her feelings of powerlessness in the face of compulsion. It's important to change the use of those judgmental terms. Instead of the word "bad," use the words "anxious" or "stressed." Instead of "good," say "in charge of your choices."

UNDERSTANDING COMPULSIVE SPENDING AND DEBTING

I am not asking you to imagine how a compulsive spender or debtor feels. You simply cannot feel his or her feelings, cravings or urges. I am sure that you have some bad habit or problem that you have been trying to get rid of . . . unsuccessfully. A common problem in our culture is procrastination. Are you someone who keeps putting things off or showing up late and hate yourself for it? Maybe you have a fear of flying and can't overcome it yet, or have been trying unhappily to give up smoking or caffeine.

The person you love who gives in to urges to spend is pretty much like you. She is not bad, nor is she acting purposely to harm you. Every time she goes on a spree it is because she is unable to cope with overwhelming feelings. She is not lacking willpower. She may be a college graduate, but she doesn't have the life-skills to deal with her problems or the feelings that result.

BE POSITIVE

Have you let your loved one's negative behavior cancel all that you find wonderful about her? See if you can remind yourself of the qualities that are lovable and her outstanding traits. She may be a capable and endearing person with a warm heart. Begin to verbally compliment her when it is valid. Be supportive. Physical support feels good too: hugs, pats on the back, and affectionate squeezes on the arm.

RECOVERY THROUGH PSYCHOTHERAPY

Compulsive spending and debting is not just a bad habit. It is a demonstration of a life out-of-balance. Self-help meetings or psychotherapy is needed to recover. The compulsive person will discover that many underlying issues must be faced, not just the negative behaviors.

Therapy for behavioral change can take a while. The therapist doesn't have a magic wand that will take it all away. If you don't see an astounding transformation in six weeks, curb your impatience. It may be best to support your friend's efforts without hovering over him. Let him be as private as he needs to about what is happening in therapy. It is none of your business.

On the other hand, your loved one may invite you to attend a session or join him in his recovery. Your initial reaction may be fear that you are going to be blamed or be the recipient of anger. Let me assure you that the therapy office is a neutral place where people can share and learn together. A skilled therapist will act as a facilitator without taking sides. You may be surprised at some things your friend or spouse can reveal to you in that safe place. You can be of great help to the one you care about by accepting the opportunity to share in the counseling experience.

PRACTICE UNCONDITIONAL ACCEPTANCE

No matter how much you want to, you cannot fix a compulsive spender or debtor. You do not have the training or expertise. Even if you belong to a recovery organization and are working on your own program, you can only change yourself. You can, however, give the gift of unconditional love and acceptance. We all want to be accepted right now as the imperfect people we are. When you accept unconditionally it means that you focus on the special inner self of the other one. You stop blaming because you know that she is worthy of love even if you don't like what she is doing.

It doesn't mean that if your wife continues to abuse your credit cards, that you continue to pay the bills. When the behavior affects you negatively, you must find a way to sort out your feelings and learn new ways to take care of yourself. There are support groups for codependents just as there is Al-Anon for those who are in relationships with alcoholics.

You may love your shopaholic friend yet find that you do not know how to control your reactions to her behavior. There are two harmful kinds of communication that helping friends often get caught in when there is an emotional crisis: blaming and discounting.

Learn to avoid blaming. Verbal insults are as bad as punches. You may be utterly frustrated because you can't help the spender or she isn't getting well fast enough. You may blurt out insults or call her names. She isn't perfect. She is doing the best she can. Her behavior often stems from low self-worth. This will not be remedied overnight. She will continue to make mistakes and have slips. When you act like a disapproving parent, she will feel guilt or shame and won't have time to examine the process that led to her compulsivity.

Blaming is dumping your feelings onto the other. Look at what those feelings really are about. Most of the time your anger and frustration comes from a feeling of powerlessness. Practice saying, "When you act compulsively, I feel powerless." Then tell the other about it. I have already advised you to stop protecting the compulsive person by holding back your feelings. It is fine to tell him that you feel frustrated, but don't beat him over the head for making you feel that way. Refrain from giving advice and offering solutions. That is rescuing again, and it will harm more than it helps. Instead, ask you friend, "What do *you* want to do about this situation?"

Discounting communication demeans the other and belittles her feelings. We are so used to hearing the phrases, "Don't be silly" or "There's nothing to worry about," that we don't realize that they are insults. If someone were to say, "How can you feel that way?" when you are worried and they aren't, how would you like that? Most of us would feel as if the person challenging us doesn't really understand. Rescuers and persecutors often tell themselves, "If that were me, I would never have done such a thing!" That's true, but your compulsive friend isn't you!

She does what she does because of how she feels. Her feelings make sense to her. She will not get better when you judge her feelings and tell her to stop feeling them. It is as if you have an itch on your back and are wriggling around trying to reach it when another person looks crossly at you and says, "Don't itch." How do you stop something that you don't feel responsible for starting? That is how the compulsive spender feels. She doesn't know how the itch to spend started. She would like to be free of it, but telling her to stop without telling her how to stop is meaningless.

WAYS YOU CAN HELP

It is important to set limits to take care of yourself when you are in a relationship with a compulsive spender or debtor. Here are some important rules for you to take to heart:

1. Don't let the spender abuse your generosity in service to her compulsion.
2. Don't give the spender your credit cards.
3. Don't co-sign any financial contract.
4. Don't be a "binge buddy" and go on spending sprees with your friend.
5. Set limits and don't back down . . . no matter what.

You are not responsible for how or when your compulsive friend or loved one recovers. All you need to do is concentrate on being a true friend. Practice the fine art of listening. Listening doesn't mean that while the other is telling you his problems you are busily thinking up what you are going to tell him to set him straight or offer new solutions. A good listener is someone who is genuinely attentive. It means you learn to be a mirror. It takes practice to let go of your judgmental ideas and become neutral.

Here are some steps to take to improve your listening skills:

1. Look at your friend while he talks to you.
2. Stay focused on his words and facial expressions.
3. Respond by repeating his statements back to him in slightly different words. It is okay to say, "Let me see if I understand what you are telling me . . ."
4. Refrain from analyzing and responding until your friend seems satisfied or has created his solution.

Here are two examples of the wrong way to listen and the right way:

WRONG:

Friend: My Visa is at its maximum and I can't even afford my monthly payment!
You: How could you let yourself get so in debt?

Loose Change

Friend: I don't know. I just can't seem to get caught up.

You: You've been saying that for years.

Friend: Well, just when I start to budget, there's always an emergency.

You: Why don't you see if you can get a loan?

Friend: Yes, but my credit isn't any good.

You: Why don't you consider bankruptcy?

Friend: Yes, but it would really set me back, and what would people think?

In this exchange you are doing all the work, and your friend is allowed to keep being the victim.

RIGHT:

Friend: My Visa is at its maximum and I can't even afford my monthly payment.

You: It sounds like you are in a real jam.

Friend: Yes, I don't know where I will find the money to pay my bills.

You: What a dilemma!

Friend: What should I do?

You: I can see that you are puzzled about what to do. What do you think you could do?

Friend: I don't know.

You: Think about it for a minute.

Friend: Maybe I can get a consolidated loan.

You: So, you are thinking about putting all your debts together.

Friend: I'm not sure I could qualify.

(after a few more interchanges between you)

Friend: What about those financial advisers who help
       you get out of debt? That's what I need. Some-
       one who knows what to do and will help me
       stay on a plan.

You: It looks to me as if that idea makes you feel
     good. It sounds like it just might be a great
     solution.

In the second dialogue, as your friend talks about
his frustration and fear, he asked you to solve the
problem for him. This will happen frequently in your
conversations. Do not rise to the bait. Use the magic
question: "What would *you* like to do about it?" Without
stopping to think, he will usually reply "I don't know."
Don't fret; just say, "Think about it for a moment;
what do you think you can do about it?" With a little
practice you will soon be able to parry all attempts to
get you to take responsibility. Eventually you will
discover that you are less stressed than when you felt
responsible for helping and solving the other's problems.

I cannot guarantee that the one you love will overcome her compulsion to spend or debt. Even if she is
in a Twelve-Step group or psychotherapy, human progress is often two steps forward and one step back.
Slips and relapses do take place. She may not get well
in the time you expect. If you put pressure on her, it
will be even more difficult for her to succeed.

One uncomfortable question you must ask yourself
is: Can I accept this person as she is *today* (that she
may never change)? If the answer in your heart is no,

you must consider that the best way to help her and yourself is to end the relationship.

If you have decided to stand by your friend or family member, here are some things you will need to think about and practice:

1. Remind yourself that you can't "fix" the other person.
2. Encourage the spender to find professional help or a self-help group.
3. Involve yourself by reading about the problem or consulting with an expert.
4. Recognize compulsive spending or debting as a sign or symptom of other conflicts in the person's life that he or she isn't coping with.
5. Stop discounting or belittling the other's feelings.
6. Stop policing the person's actions or punishing the other.
7. Stop rescuing the other or backing down when there is conflict.
8. Learn how to listen in a loving way.
9. Practice unconditional acceptance and love.

FACE YOUR FEARS

Although my suggestions about refraining from persecuting and rescuing make sense to you, you may feel hesitant about putting them into action because of your fears. One common fear is that the loved one will be ruined financially or even go to prison because of dubious practices or writing bad checks.

If you are married to a compulsive spender or debtor you may feel afraid that the other will cause your ruin or destroy your credit rating. As long as you pay his or her bills and share a joint account or credit card with that person you are in jeopardy. You may feel powerless to stop your spouse's behavior and believe that there is nothing else you can do. Stop letting your fear control you. Seek the advice of a lawyer or accountant to see what steps you can take to protect yourself.

When the spender doesn't heed your advice you will often feel angry. You think, "If he loved me, he would stop spending all our money and start saving." The person with the spending disorder isn't going to get better to please you. You did not cause the problem nor can you make it go away.

You may have to look more closely at yourself. When you allow your frustration and anger to build up, you usually will be blaming the other for causing it. Yet you have chosen this other person to relate to or be married to. When you feel scared, helpless, or enraged, does this remind you of other relationships in your life? Is this anything like the way your parents interacted? Looking at why you feel good when you are rescuing another or feeling so angry it is okay to punish another is a challenge that may enrich your life.

LEARNING TO FORGIVE

It is easy to talk about forgiving, but it is very difficult to actually do after you have been hurt by the other person's behavior and attitudes. Forgiveness is possible when you cancel the debt you think the other person owes you . . . living up to your expectations.

When you allow yourself to let go of those expectations and fantasies and accept your friend as he really is, flawed and imperfect, you do not have to walk away from him. Support him in a new way, free of criticism or rescuing. If you don't know how to be in this new type of relationship, you may want to join a group such as Codependents Anonymous or consult with a therapist.

You can forgive when the old hurts and angers of the past are cleared away. It is never too late to heal a relationship. Each of us wants to be loved and cherished for who we are right now. This moment we are lovable though we have many shortcomings and problems. Your friend is just like you except that she copes with the pain of her life in a different way, by spending or debting. When you learn to understand and love her, you also will be learning to accept and love yourself more.

SUGGESTED READINGS

Assagioli, Roberto. *Psychosynthesis*. New York: Viking, 1971.

_____. *Act of Will*. New York: Viking, 1973.

Beattie, Melody. *Codependent No More*. Harper/Hazelden, 1987.

Beck, Aaron T. *Cognitive Therapy and the Emotional Disorders*. New York: Meridian, 1976.

Bradshaw, John. *Healing the Shame that Binds You*. Deerfield Beach, FL: Health Communications, 1988.

Burns, David D. Feeling Good: *The New Mood Therapy*. New York: Morrow, 1980.

Damon, Janet E. *Shopaholics*. Los Angeles: Price Stern Sloan, 1988.

Engel, Lewis and Tom Ferguson. *Imaginary Crimes*. Boston: Houghton Mifflin, 1990.

Gillies, Jerry. *Money-Love*. New York: Warner Books, 1978.

Goldberg, Herbert, and Robert T. Lewis. *Money Madness*. New York: William Morrow, 1978.

Goleman, Daniel. *Vital Lies, Simple Truths*. New York: Simon & Schuster, 1985.

Hatterer, Lawrence J. *The Pleasure Addicts*. New York: A.S. Barnes, 1980.

Hodgson, Ray and Peter Miller. *Self Watching*. New York: Facts on File, 1982.

James, Muriel and Dorothy Jongeward. *Born to Win*. Reading, MA: Addison-Wesley, 1971.

Lazarus, Arnold and Allen Fay. *I Can if I Want To*. New York: Warner Books, 1975.

Lieberman, Annette and Vicki Lindner. *Unbalanced Accounts*. New York: The Atlantic Monthly Press, 1987.

Marlatt, G. Alan and Judith Gordon. *Relapse Prevention*. New York: Guilford Press, 1985.

Milkman, Harvey and Stanley Sunderwirth. *Craving for Ecstasy*. Lexington, MA: Lexington Books, 1987.

Mundis, Jerrold. *How to Get Out of Debt, Stay Out of Debt and Live Prosperously*. New York: Bantam Books, 1988.

Peele, Stanton. *Diseasing of America*. Lexington MA: Lexington Books, 1989.

Schaef, Ann Wilson. *When Society Becomes an Addict*. San Francisco: Harper & Row, 1987.

_____ *Co-Dependence: Misunderstood-Mistreated*. San Francisco: Harper & Row, 1986.

Siegel, Ronald K. *Intoxication: Life in Pursuit of Artificial Paradise*. New York: E.F. Dutton, 1989.

Stone, Elizabeth. *Black Sheep and Kissing Cousins*. New York: Times Books, 1988.

Wesson, Carolyn. *Women Who Shop Too Much*. New York: St. Martin's Press, 1990.